IN SEARCH OF GOD

IN SEARCH OF GOD

CONRAD SIMONSON

A PILGRIM PRESS BOOK
from United Church Press, Philadelphia

Library of Congress Cataloging in Publication Data

Simonson, Conrad.
  In search of God.

  "A Pilgrim Press book."
  Bibliography: p.
  1. God. I. Title.
BT102.S516   231   73-19728
ISBN 0-8298-0256-8

United Church Press, 1505 Race Street,
Philadelphia, Pennsylvania 19102

To my fathers and grandfathers
Who tried everything
Who knew a song when they heard one
And who named their dream God.

To my children
Heidi, Gail, Kathryn, and Paul
Who were born in the world
Into which I immigrated.

Contents

Preface

This is a book about God. It is also a book about us, and what we have meant when we said God, and what we might mean. The book is a kind of pilgrimage. If you could read it as I would wish you to, you would read it all, all at once, and then hold the pieces together and think about them. The next best thing would be to start here and read straight through to the end.

It pleases me to remember that there are people whom I love to whom great portions of gratitude and gladness are due. Let me list some of them:

Margaret: Dear Margaret. All she has gotten out of this book are two cats—Pooka and Narcissus Anderson—and she did not even want them. The children did, so I brought them home from Chicago on one of my trips there to write in the middle of the night in a friendly library. The cats eat houseplants.

Cyndy Klinksiek and Marsha Bergen: May every teacher have students like Marsha and Cyndy! They met with me regularly to try all these ideas for size and texture, to look skeptical or grin with delight. Cyndy always got the best chair; Marsha always came a little late.

The Religion Department at Luther College: With them I discussed the basic premise of this book, and they, almost to a man, took strenuous issue with the thesis. (It may happen that they will someday want to thank me for that statement.)

Everyone in the library at Lutheran School of Theology at Chicago: Particular thanks are due to Joel Lundeen and

9

Lowell Albee, who are always helpful and who made the fine resources and facilities of the library available to me.

I want to make it perfectly clear that while everyone was helpful and inspirational and long-suffering, I claim all the credit for whatever good lies here and accept none of the blame for whatever proves to be shoddy thinking. The rewards for writing books are small enough, without having forever to agree with everything one says.

CHAPTER 1

On Behalf
of
the Fool

Some things are nearly impossible to believe.

I speak of world views.

It is probably a function of our own intelligence that we drive toward coherence, toward an overview of everything we know. It is a kind of map making. The term world view is used almost exclusively to apply to those largest things we know, those ideas within which unnumbered particulars are given perspective. I believe, for instance, that the earth is more or less round. It doesn't really look round as I stand on it and walk up and down on it, but for an uncounted number of sometimes abstract and sometimes sophisticated reasons, I am convinced that roundness accounts best for what I know about the earth. The contentions of the Flat Earth Society fly in the face of so many particular things I know about the world that I can scarcely conceive of taking seriously the notion that the earth is flat. The plain fact is, though, that once nearly everybody *did* believe the earth was flat, and within the large perspective that world view gave them it was scarcely possible to think any other way. That change of world view, like every change of world views, demanded massive relocations of mental things.

In 1941 Rudolf Bultmann read an address titled "New Testament and Mythology" to a group of pastors, in which he said that the world view of the New Testament was not an option for modern men. The world of angels and demons, of heaven above and hell below, of miracles and divine and demonic interventions in the ordinary affairs of the world was incredible. And to the extent that people today are asked to affirm Christianity as it is expressed in the terms of that mythology, participation in the faith is nearly impossible: *"the kerygma is incredible to modern man, for he is convinced that the mythical view of the world is obsolete."*[1] One must ask then, Bultmann said, whether we expect converts to accept not only the gospel but also the world view in which it is set.

There is nothing particularly Christian about the world view expressed in the New Testament, Bultmann wrote. It is simply the cosmology of a prescientific age. And further, it is impossible for twentieth-century men to affirm a mythological cosmology because one does not so easily or freely choose world views. World views are determined for one by his place in history. World views do change, of course, but only when confronted by new facts so compelling as to make the previous view untenable. At that point one has no alternative but to modify one's view of the world. At the same time, Bultmann argued, it is impossible to revive an obsolete view of the world by mere fiat, and certainly not a mythical view; not for men whose world view is shaped by modern science. "It is no longer possible for anyone seriously to hold the New Testament view of the world—in fact, there is no one who does."[2]

In the strictest sense, no one does any longer hold a New Testament world view, but it is also true that for some people a scientific view of the world (if that is an adequate way to describe common contemporary ways of seeing reality) is not compatible with their religious faith. For those people, insofar as they are able, the New Testament world view is tenable, if only for the purpose of thinking theologically. But for daily life, modern men really are shaped by science. They have no choice. "Therefore, it is mere wishful thinking to suppose that the ancient world-view of the Bible can be renewed."[3]

Because world views *do* change, there are times, both in general history and in particular lives, when two world views compete. That is very common in individual lives. The church regularly finds itself declaring its faith in terms of a world view—or, less broadly, in terms of a science—from an earlier time. That may be for several reasons. In the first place, the fact that world views do change has not always been recognized, probably because those changes do not often occur. Even when they do occur, they have not always been recognized for what they are. It is true, too, that theology is often regarded as the expression of eternal truths, truths that, once expressed in certain ways or within certain categories, must be defended against modification. The unchanging creed seems somehow a guarantee of unchanging truth. In the book *Custer Died for Your Sins,* Vine Deloria, Jr., tells of the fear that Christians sometimes show of losing Christian truth when new forms of expression and world view are entered:

A Navajo interpreter was asked to demonstrate how the missionary's sermon was translated into Navajo. So the white missionary gave a few homilies and the interpreter spoke a few words of Navajo. The trainees cooed with satisfaction that meaning could actually be transferred into a barbaric tongue like Navajo.

One missionary was skeptical, however, and asked if there were specific words in Navajo that were comparable to English words. He was afraid, he said, that the wrong messages might be transmitted. So he asked what the Navajo word for "faith" was. Quickly the Navajo replied with the desired word.

"Yes," the missionary commented, "that's all very nice. Now what does that word mean?"

"Faith," said the Navajo, smiling.[4]

And sometimes it seems to Christians responsible for the articulation and defense of the faith that alternate world views simply are wrong, necessitating denial. So, whether for conscious or unconscious reasons, people reared in the church often find themselves caught between older and more recent sciences or world views, unable for the time to choose between them. Of that more will be said later. For the culture generally, though, and, given enough time, for the individual too, new world views supplant older ones. When that happens, there is no longer a choice. One simply cannot deny what seems perfectly evident; world views are always evident. The world is a kind of ball in space. We all *know* that, and to deny it, or to accept as true something that necessitates the denial of it, is ludicrous. For this reason, Bultmann insisted that, unless we were willing to confine Christian faith to those few persons who are not members of contemporary culture and mentality, we must demythologize the gospel, separate it from the accidental world view in which it is biblically couched and express it in terms of our own understanding of how the world works.

In the West, at least, there are very few theologians deserving the name who take serious issue with Bultmann's articulation of the problem. Whether his particular understanding of the scientific view of the world is adequate, or whether the existential philosophy of Martin Heidegger is a satisfactory vehicle for restatement of the faith, can readily be argued. But world views do change, and for those persons who, simply because they live when and where they do, find themselves seeing the world differently than they used to, or differently than men generally used to, it is hopeless to propose a return to earlier ways of apprehending reality. They simply cannot believe in a world peppered with demonic forces any more than they can believe that ships going west will sail off the edge of the Atlantic.

In his article "The Structure of Scientific Revolutions,"[5] Thomas Kuhn examines the manner in which world views change. Kuhn does not actually use the term world view for the main thrust of his argument but speaks rather of the paradigms of science. He does not define paradigm any more closely than Bultmann defines world view, but it is evident that they mean very much the same thing. Paradigm is not so grand a word as world view—that may reflect method more than modesty—but what Kuhn says about the way new paradigms are adopted applies as well to what theologians call world views.

The most famous case of paradigm change is probably the emergence of Copernican astronomy. The Ptolemaic system, which developed in the two centuries preceding and the two following the time of Christ, was essentially a system in which the sun, moon, and planets were thought to move in great circles around the earth, which was unmoved at the center. In order to account for what seemed to be variations from perfect circular movements, the planets were believed to trace small circular movements within the paths of their larger orbits about the earth. The Ptolemaic system, once it was generally understood, was a perfectly commonsense view of the world. It was a view of the principal bodies of what we now call our solar system from the earth out. After all, that is where, until very recently, all men have stood when they looked at it. The Ptolemaic system was admirably successful in predicting the position of both planets and stars. For some purposes, the Ptolemaic system is still serviceable. But the system is not perfect, and in time it was noted that the Ptolemaic predictions never quite precisely matched the best available observations. With every discrepancy, Ptolemaic astronomers tried to make minute adjustments in Ptolemy's system of compounded circles; but with increasingly accurate measurements adjustments in one place tended to produce larger discrepancies in another. The Ptolemaic model is what Kuhn calls a paradigm. It is a way of seeing reality or, if that is too large a term, of seeing the world in its context. In its time, the Ptolemaic paradigm was sufficiently convincing to attract adherents from competing models for scientific activity. At the same time it was sufficiently open-ended to leave all sorts of problems for continuing research. In its time, Ptolemaic astronomy constituted normal science.[6]

Because of repeated outside interruption and because, in the absence of printing, communication between astronomers was restricted, the difficulties in the Ptolemaic system were not always quickly recognized and commonly incorporated into a revised system. But by the time of Copernicus, in the sixteenth century, the Ptolemaic system was both cumbersome and demonstrably inaccurate. When Copernicus proposed, in effect, to see the system from the sun out, he was proposing another paradigm, another model for seeing the world and nearby celestial bodies. Today we take a solar system for granted, but that by no means reflects the situation in the sixteenth century. When he proposed it, Copernicus' way of seeing the world was neither simpler nor noticeably more accurate than the system of Ptolemy. Those kinds of results came only after long observation and recalculation by men who accepted the Copernican paradigm.

The real situation, when a new paradigm is proposed, is that of consternation and confusion. Paradigms shape one's expectations and even determine what one sees; the prospect of a completely other way of seeing things is extremely disturbing. Kuhn cites a psychological study:

In a psychological experiment that deserves to be far better known outside the trade, Bruner and Postman asked experimental subjects to identify on short and controlled exposure a series of playing cards. Many of the cards were normal, but some were made anomalous, e.g., a red six of spades and a black four of hearts. Each experimental run was constituted by the display of a single card to a single subject in a series of gradually increased exposures. After each exposure the subject was asked what he had seen, and the run was terminated by two successive correct identifications.

Even on the shortest exposures many subjects identified most of the cards, and after a small increase all the subjects identified them all. For the normal cards these identifications were usually correct, but the anomalous cards were almost always identified, without apparent hesitation or puzzlement, as normal. The black four of hearts might, for example, be identified as the four of either spades or hearts. Without any awareness of trouble, it was immediately fitted to one of the conceptual categories prepared by prior experience. One would not even like to say that the subjects had seen something different from what they identified. With a further increase of exposure to the anomalous cards, subjects did begin to hesitate and to display awareness of anomaly. Exposed, for example, to the red six of spades, some would say: That's the six of spades, but there's something wrong with it—the black has a red border. Further increase of exposure resulted in still more hesitation and confusion until finally, and sometimes quite suddenly, most subjects would produce the correct identification without hesitation. Moreover, after doing this with two or three of the anomalous cards, they would have little further difficulty with the others. A few subjects, however, were never able to make the requisite adjustment of their categories. Even at forty times the average exposure required to recognize normal cards for what they were, more than 10 per cent of the anomalous cards were not correctly identified. And the subjects who then failed often experienced acute personal distress. One of them exclaimed: "I can't make the suit out, whatever it is. It didn't even look like a card that time. I don't know what color it is now or whether it's a spade or a heart. I'm not even sure now what a spade looks like. My God!"[7]

"What a man sees," Kuhn says, "depends both upon what he looks at and also upon what his previous visual-conceptual experience has taught him to see."[8]

"The decision to reject one paradigm is always simultaneously the decision to accept another, and the judgment leading to that decision involves the comparison of both paradigms with nature *and* with each other."[9] To use the illustration already given, when Ptolemaic and Copernican paradigms conflicted, one of the steps taken to determine the validity of the claims of each was to compare each paradigm with the direct observation of the celestial bodies themselves. Unfortunately, in the early stages of the conflict that procedure often does not resolve the issue. The Ptolemaic system, for instance, was already plagued with inconsistencies, and the Copernican system was still so unrefined that it displayed as many irregularities as the other. The second step, that of comparing the paradigms with each other, is no less frustrating. "When paradigms enter, as they must, into a debate about paradigm choice, their role is necessarily circular. Each group uses its own paradigm to argue in that paradigm's defense."[10] Persuasion becomes the sole force of the argument. One can only provide a clear exhibit of what scientific practice will be like for those who adopt the new view of nature. "It cannot be made logically or even probabilistically compelling for those who refuse to step into the circle."[11]

In a conflict of paradigms, some men do, in a kind of conversion experience, see everything differently. Anomalies and crises within the context of the old system are terminated,

not by deliberation and interpretation, but by a relatively sudden and unstructured event like the gestalt switch. Scientists then often speak of the "scales falling from the eyes" or of the "lightning flash" that "inundates" a previously obscure puzzle, enabling its components to be seen in a new way that for the first time permits its solution.[12]

Further, Kuhn argues, the transition between paradigms cannot be made one deliberate step at a time, logically and neutrally. It occurs at once (although not instantly) or not at all. In that respect, the scientific process that Kuhn describes has religious parallels. "William James cites a convert at a rural revival meeting who testified to a sudden perception of glory in his hogs: 'When I came to myself . . . oh, how I was changed, and everything became new. My horses and hogs and even everybody seemed changed.' "[13] And Max Planck said that "a new scientific truth does not triumph by convincing its opponents and making them see the light, but rather because its opponents eventually die, and a new generation grows up that is familiar with it."[14] Similar statements have been made about the manner in which philosophy proceeds: new philosophies do not refute their predecessors, they ignore them. The transfer of allegiance from one paradigm to another, Kuhn says, is a conversion experience.[15] The fact is, then, that some people never see the new way and that, particularly in science, most of the supporters of new paradigms are either young or new to their fields.[16] In the field of art, Gertrude Stein, writing about Picasso, said, "To see the things in a new way, that is really difficult, everything prevents one, habits, schools, daily life, reason, the necessities of daily life, indolence, everything prevents one. . . ."[17] The person who shifts his allegiance to a new paradigm at an early stage in its acceptance must often do so, not because the new paradigm solves all the problems, but because it solves a few and holds promise for solving many others. "A decision of that kind can only be made on faith."[18]

"I saw this familiar—too *familiar*—fact at a different angle, and I was charmed and haunted by it."[19]

When Rudolf Bultmann proposed to demythologize the New Testament, he was in fact saying that while we see reality differently from first-century Christians, it is the same reality. To use an expression from Kuhn again, "The man who first saw the exterior of the box from above later sees its interior from below."[20] Bultmann professed to be unable to see demons and angels and eternal places, but in a peculiar kind of way he did see God. In fact, he insisted that God could *not* be demythologized. "It is often said," Bultmann wrote, "that it is impossible to carry through de-mythologizing consistently, since, if the message of the New Testament is to be retained at all, we are bound to speak of God as acting."[21] The kerygma, as Bultmann understood it, was the affirmation that God has *acted,* and the world—this world—has come to an end, and man has become something new.[22] There remains one miracle for Bultmann, and that miracle is the action of God in the world: the Word became flesh. Bultmann stoutly insisted that God could not be demythologized.

In an early essay on liberal theology, Bultmann had said, "The subject of theology is *God*, and the chief charge to be brought against liberal theology is that it has dealt not with God but with man."[23] Bultmann never wavered from that position. In contrast to Ludwig Feuerbach, for instance, Bultmann never proposed that talk about God is *just* talk about man. He did not translate theology into anthropology. "The subject of theology is *God*." Bultmann did agree that talk about God was *at the same time* talk about man. From the perspective of an observer, the action of God is hidden. God does not act *between* events but *within* them. "Only the so-called natural, secular (worldly) events are visible to every man and capable of proof. It is *within* them that God's hidden action is taking place."[24] To speak of God as acting within events, Bultmann freely admits, is not an assertion accessible to scientific analysis. In that respect, Bultmann does not agree that science is entirely adequate to describe human experience. Faith is not accessible to science, and faith is the assertion of concourse between God and man. The scientific world view cannot comprehend that faith experience, however usefully it may serve for a general understanding of the world. "The action of God is hidden from every eye except the eye of faith."[25]

From that general position Bultmann concludes that the only statements about God which are legitimate are statements about the existential relation between God and man. Faith

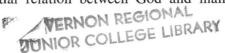

statements are by definition existential statements. It is not possible, then, to assert actions of God in the cosmos, since they simply are not accessible to men.

The affirmation that God is creator cannot be a theoretical statement about God as *creator mundi* in a general sense. The affirmation can only be a personal confession that I understand myself to be a creature which owes its existence to God. It cannot be made a neutral statement, but only as thanksgiving and surrender.[26]

From a scientific point of view, one cannot speak of an act of God. Faith statements are "nevertheless" statements. Events in nature and history, completely accountable to scientific analysis, are *nevertheless* understood in faith to be the actions of God.[27]

It is fair, then, Bultmann admits, to ask whether statements about God are *simply* statements about man. Does divine reality have any objective reality at all? Does it exist apart from subjective experience? Is not faith, then, simply reduced to human experience? Is God only an inner event in the soul? "That God cannot be seen apart from faith," Bultmann says, "does not mean that he does not exist apart from it."[28] If faith were demonstrable, it would not be faith. "For if it were susceptible to proof it would mean that we could know and establish God apart from faith, and that would be placing him on a level with the world of tangible, objective reality. In that realm we are certainly justified in demanding proof."[29] God can only be believed upon in defiance of all outward appearance. "The man who wishes to believe in God as his God must realize that he has nothing in his hand on which to base his faith. He is suspended in mid-air, and cannot demand a proof of the Word which addresses him."[30] God can be believed only because of, and in spite of, experience. Norman Perrin, possibly the best post-Bultmannian scholar in America, says:

To return to our main point: it follows from what we have said that God cannot be the effective cause of an event within history; only a man or a people's faith in God can be that. Moreover, since the process of history is uniform and not random—if it were random any kind of historical existence would become impossible

—then it follows that there never has been and there never will be an event within history (that is, world history) of which God has been or will be the effective cause. Many people shrink from this conclusion and perhaps most Christians and Jews would do so. But Bultmann does not shrink from it.*

Bultmann's position backs him into an impossible corner. There are no scientifically verifiable experiences of God. God cannot be seen acting in nature or history generally. Bultmann also wants to insist that there are *personal*, or existential, confrontations with God, but because of his unrelenting honesty, he is compelled to admit that those personal confrontations with God are indistinguishable from illusion. "It is clear, on the one hand, that faith, speaking of God as acting, cannot defend itself against the charge of being an illusion, and, on the other hand, that faith does not mean a psychologically subjective event."[31] One is left, then, in the position of accepting the word of the believer that certain experiences, which are indistinguishable from illusion, are not illusion but encounters with God and that "faith" is the name of the certainty which makes such claims of encounter with God. In that respect, Bultmann is solidly in the company of the liberal theologians whose enterprise he wished to deny: as with Friedrich Schleiermacher, the religious experience is withdrawn to the realm of the inner life; and whether that inner life be profound feelings or moral imperative or passionate and private conviction, there is no way for either the believer himself or for the observer to distinguish those inner life experiences from pure and simple illusion. As Thomas Hobbes commented, "To say he hath spoken to him in a dream, is no more than to say he dreamed that God spake to him. . . ."[32]

How did Bultmann get into that corner? He got there because he insisted that God was not a mythological concept and that God *does* act, even though every event is understandable without recourse to God as an explanation. To assert God in that way is indistinguishable from asserting nothing at all.

At least since Schleiermacher, the dilemma for theology has been how to assert an unequivocal knowledge of God. God is

---

* From the book *The Promise of Bultmann* by Norman Perrin, pp. 90-91. Copyright © 1969, by Norman Perrin. Reprinted by permission of J. B. Lippincott Company.

plainly seen neither in nature nor in scripture nor, in spite of either Schleiermacher or Bultmann, in the arena of personal experience. Sigmund Freud taught us how deceptive feelings can be. There may be a simpler explanation: perhaps there is no God.

In a recent book, Alistair Kee distinguishes between faith and belief. "Ours is an age of faith," he says, "but not belief."[33] Kee understands faith to mean commitment, with ultimate concern.[34] One may choose whether or not to commit oneself to something, to some great cause or to Jesus, for instance. On the other hand, Kee says, "it is not generally recognized by religious people that while a man may choose to have faith, he cannot choose belief."[35] Belief, Kee says, depends on the culture in which one is raised, and belief is adequate as its concepts and categories to interpret and explain our experience are adequate. One may decide to have faith in something, but one cannot decide to believe something. At first reading, Kee's distinction between faith and belief is not clear, probably because common usage does not closely and consistently adhere to the distinction Kee intends. Once it is recognized, however, that Kee uses belief very much as other people use the term world view, his argument comes into closer focus. Further, Kee uses belief to indicate not every conceivable world view but particularly in reference to a religious world view and, by implication, a *prior* religious world view. His usage of the term is not entirely consistent, but along the lines suggested here his argument is clear. For instance:

It is not generally recognized by religious people that while a man may choose to have faith [i.e., may choose to commit himself], he cannot choose his belief [his world view]. What we believe [our world view]—about ourselves, our society, our world—depends on the culture in which we are raised.[36]

Like Bultmann, Kee insists, then, that world views are given and evident and not optional, as is faith or commitment. Beliefs, or world views, are shaped by the age in which one lives, and only in a time of changing world views do most people "choose" between them. "To demand faith is one thing, to require belief is quite another, since changing our beliefs is not something that can be brought about by an act of will."[37]

Our particular time in history, Kee maintains, is character-ized by faith (commitment), but not by belief (a religious world view). "In particular, belief in God has disappeared, at least as an effective element of contemporary living."[38] The problem for contemporary man does not lie in the adequacy of this or that conception of God, but whether any conception of God corresponds to anything in our experience. It is not simply that traditional theism is no longer adequate; "rather the crisis stems from the fact that there is an absence of any experience which could be interpreted as experience of God."[39]

That is to say, the concept God is an inherent part of a world view, a world view that is foreign to many contemporary people. One cannot choose against what seems to be common sense to adopt a religious world view (one that includes God) if one's own experience is that everything is better understood otherwise. God is not one to whom one commits oneself; God is a way of comprehending reality that is no longer meaningful for some men, any more than is a flat earth or an earth-centered cosmology.

In a religious age men have religious beliefs [world views], that is, they interpret and explain the world in its own terms. Ours is a secular age, and that is why in our time *all* religious beliefs have become problematic, especially belief in God. And if belief in God is the presupposition, the prior condition of Christianity, then Christian belief will not be possible in our secular age. . . .

I am therefore proposing an understanding of Christian faith, appropriate to our secular age, which does not require belief in God as its prior condition.[40]

It is precisely at the point where Kee proposes an under-standing of Christian faith without belief in God that he finds himself at odds with Rudolf Bultmann. Bultmann, Kee sug-gests, focused demythologization on the wrong issues. "A final stumbling block has been overlooked by Bultmann and his critics, which prevents modern man from coming to terms with the gospel of Jesus Christ. . . . That stumbling block is God."[41]

The issue at stake is whether God is a way of looking at and explaining the world, an *outmoded* way of looking at and explaining the world, or whether God exists in himself, apart from any particular world view. If God is, in effect, a world view or part of a world view, it is inappropriate—even impossible—to call for commitment to that view. If, on the other hand, God exists apart from a mythological, scientific, or any other world view, and is in some kind of relationship with men, then men might be asked, reasonably enough, to trust God, to commit themselves to God, to have faith in God. Bultmann, as we have seen, was very careful to exclude the concept of God from the business of demything. Kee insists that God is an intrinsic part of one way—a religious way—of interpreting experience and for that reason is as open a concept for reinterpretation as the shape of space, for instance.

Almost everyone agrees that God is not experienced directly, immediately, unequivocally. Bultmann had agreed that whenever one claimed an experience of God, it was always possible for that event to be interpreted as a mere illusion. The believer, of course, denies that, but empirically one has only the *contention* of the believer that God has spoken or acted or whatever. "We can believe in God only in spite of experience."[42] As Alistair Kee puts it, "There is no direct experience of God, only experiences which are interpreted in a religious manner."[43] Of course, when Kee says that, he is not precisely agreeing with Bultmann. They agree only to the extent that there are no self-evident or scientifically ascertainable or unequivocal experiences of God. Bultmann thinks that the lack of objective proof for God is not a weakness but is the strength of faith,[44] although what that assertion can mean is not at all clear. It seems to be a peculiar way of saying that people with no objectively ascertainable evidence for God can nevertheless be very convinced that there is a God. But that begs the issue. One is, at that point, back at the beginning again, confronted with a claim that God is responsible for experiences that admittedly can be interpreted without recourse to a belief in God. "Religious experience," Kee says, "means the religious interpretation of experience."[45]

It is simply the case that some people, looking at themselves and each other and the world, understand what they see as the handiwork of God, as evidence of his great wisdom and unending care and limitless design. Contrary to much uninformed opinion, such religious people, looking at the world, do *not* take what they see to be *proof* for God. Proofs for God have been very few, almost always cautiously applied, and universally unconvincing. Proofs for God almost always begin with faith in God and seek only to understand what is already believed. It is also simply and undeniably the case that other people, looking at themselves and each other and the world, understand what they see without recourse to God. All the same phenomena that believers in God appeal to are, for this second group, understood from a different perspective. It is precisely like Ptolemaic and Copernican astronomers, each beginning with a certain mind-set, seeing the same phenomena and wondering why the other cannot perceive what seems evident.

Once it was the case almost everybody saw reality from a God perspective. God was assumed. God was a world view. As Kee uses the term, God was a belief. That is no longer so. Today there are many people who simply do not "see" that way. Atheists is not a good word for them, insofar as that word has a campaign character to it.

We do not speak of "a-unicornists," to refer to those who do not believe in unicorns. No one qualifies for that title, since no one thinks there is anything to deny in the first place. The contemporary situation is, I believe, similar with respect to belief in God. In the strict sense of the word, there are few a-theists going around today for the simple reason that it does not occur to a large number of people that there is anything to deny. . . . The majority of people today are atheists not because certain "difficulties" prevent them from believing in God, but because there is nothing in their experience which might lead them to suspect that there is a God.[46]

In another culture, in another time in history, in which God was an almost universal way of looking at reality, in which God was as commonly accepted and understood as the belief that the earth was flat or that space was geocentric, it was only a fool who denied God. Fools are those who deny what is self-evident, who do not commonly understand. For many, many people, that is still so. God is the way they perceive reality, and from where they stand, and in terms of how they see, only a fool could deny what they affirm. In fact, the world has no shortage of profoundly religious people who assert, sometimes remorsefully and sometimes belligerently, that people who do not see the world as they do—that is, with God as the ultimate and essential explanation for reality—will be absolutely damned for their alternate understandings of experience. That is an impossible demand, even perverse. The question is whether the term God corresponds to anything in our experience. For a significant number of contemporary men, it does not. To ask those people to believe in God is not like asking them to believe that God is fair and just and loving and to be trusted. If they saw reality that way—if they believed in God —they might well trust God to be fair and just and kind. But they have no experience of God at all. "The character of contemporary atheism is the absence of anything which could justifiably be interpreted as experience of a subject of personal encounter, a subject with whom a relationship is possible."[47] To ask them to believe in God is not the Reformation assertion that God is forgiving to those who trust him; it rather is asking for an exchange of world views. One might as well ask for belief that the earth is flat. It is impossible to believe. One cannot go back that way. It may be that the contemporary world view—a secular world view[48]—is inadequate, and that someday we will see ourselves and each other and the world altogether differently than we do now. Perhaps so. But one may be quite certain that we shall not go back to Ptolemy, and for many Christians neither can we go back to God.

It is important to note that for many *Christians* God is no longer an option. The subtitle of Kee's book is *Christian Faith Without Belief in God.* Christians commonly come to that situation in two ways. Some have grown up in the Christian church, having been taught and having accepted a belief in God as an inherent and indispensable part of their faith. The way in which Jesus is spoken of, or, more precisely, the way in which Jesus is *evaluated,* is almost solely in terms of God-language. There is very little room in terms of traditional Christianity to speak of Jesus apart from God. It has often been maintained, however accurately, that most ordinary

Christians think of Jesus as a divine being who posed as a human being for a time, or who even participated in some wondrous way in the human condition, but who now has returned to his divine beginning place, perhaps somewhat changed for his experience but clearly divine. For some Christians, though, who have learned about Jesus that way, the identification of Jesus with divinity is no longer possible. It is not for them just a matter of keeping a proper balance between his humanity and his divinity, as theologians have generally urged believers to do. It is, rather, that God no longer makes sense to them, but Jesus does. On the other hand, there are people who have not come to their interest or commitment to Jesus through traditional Christian ways at all. They are those who find Jesus to be a captivatingly fascinating man, even at this great historical distance, but who cannot for a moment affirm the world view in which Jesus lived and which Jesus accepted, which the biblical writers presupposed when they wrote of Jesus, and in which Christian theology has articulated its commitment to Jesus. Nevertheless, they are ready, often in ways that are not carefully and precisely expressed, to affirm Jesus as the way and the truth and the life, as the one who is most important for their understanding of life generally, who is definitive for their self-understanding and commitment. But of God in any traditional and ordinary sense they know and need nothing. As Kee puts it, "He would be a Christian if he took as his ultimate concern what came to expression in Jesus Christ. What could it add if he believed also in God?"[49] That may be an unhappy way to say it. The term Christ is obviously tied to theistic conceptions, and whether it is appropriate to use a Tillichian term like "ultimate concern" in a time better described by relativities than absolutes must be argued separately. The sense is clear. There are people who are willing to call themselves Christians, willing to commit themselves to the kind of life that Christians have always said is inherent in Christian commitment, who simply cannot entertain notions about God. God is not the way they see reality; Jesus is.

Much work remains to be done. What it means to commit oneself to Jesus as the way and the truth and the life (to use very traditional language) needs to be explored. The world didn't change when someone said it was round, nor did the universe change shape when someone else said it was not geocentric. Men changed. They changed the way they saw. Their world views changed. Jesus did believe in God. He also believed in demons and a quick and traumatic end to the world and, one may suppose, a geocentric universe (everybody did). Most Christians in history have believed in God, too. Now some don't, not because they choose not to commit themselves to God's rule but because they do not find God to be an appropriate way to regard reality. Rudolf Bultmann stoutly maintained that demythologization was not a reductive process, in which myth was simply subtracted from biblical materials. Myth, he said, must be interpreted, not deleted. Perhaps that is the way forward with the term God, too. People who used the term *meant* something. What they meant needs to be analyzed, because the world of which they spoke is still there, and they were saying something about it.

CHAPTER 2

A Void,
and Darkness
over the Deep

God has died in *our* time," Thomas Altizer said, "in *our* history, in *our* existence."[1] It wasn't official, though, until *Time* magazine confirmed it.[2] Rereading that 1966 *Time* article is a curious business. "Is God Dead?" was the cover caption. It was *Time's* first nonpictorial cover that attracted popular attention, and which was widely understood to be a statement rather than a question. The article itself was titled "Toward a Hidden God." Hidden gods are not necessarily dead gods, as our subsequent experience has suggested. It is not at all evident, from a reading of those theologians who write of God's death, or of the situation after the death of God, that *death* is really what they mean or that it is of *God's* death that they speak. The theologians are not alone. There is a sense in which the *Time* article represents the first public acknowledgement of a general state of mind regarding God, although there had been a number of earlier publications. Citing a Lou Harris poll from late 1965, *Time* said that 97 percent of American citizens said they believed in God—hardly fertile ground for planting a theological revolt against the idea of God. But at the same time, only 27 percent of that group of

29

professed believers called themselves deeply religious. Presumably the other believers in God were only moderately or mildly religious, suggesting that, whatever the degree of religion, some kind of belief in God was a common denominator. That was 1965. The newer question is whether belief in God is necessary for religious faith. For ages we have assumed so. The largest theological question before us is what we mean when we say God, and what then the death of God is about.

Earlier that same year Thomas Altizer and William Hamilton had provided a list of at least ten things that the death of God might mean.[3] They suggested that they were not rehearsing simple atheism, claiming that there is no God and never has been. They proposed, instead, that they were atheists with a difference: "That there once was a God to whom adoration, praise and trust were appropriate, possible, and even necessary, but that now there is no such God."[4] It is difficult to understand how William Hamilton could assent to that definition of the movement, since it is a description much more appropriate to Altizer's theology. One can surely say that Altizer and Hamilton must have understood that description of the death of God in two different ways. For Altizer the death of God is a name for something that happened to God as well as to us, but it is hard to imagine how Hamilton could assert that as a description of something God has done, unless it is the case (as we might reasonably suspect) that something like the "hiddenness" of God is true of Hamilton's later position as well as of his first writings.

There are other possibilities. It may be that the idea of God and the name God are in need of radical reformulation. It may be that we need a new name for God, or perhaps just a decent silence. The faint echo of Dietrich Bonhoeffer is heard here, as he often is in Hamilton's writings. Several months before his letters reveal what he termed "surprising" and "worrisome" thoughts, Bonhoeffer had already begun to wonder if we talk about God too easily: "The fact that the Israelites *never* uttered the name of God always makes me think, and I can understand it better as I go on."[5] And later he confessed that it made him uncomfortable to talk about God with religious people whose "God" he disavowed.

In the same sense, it might be true that our traditional theological and liturgical language needs a complete overhaul. That is affirmed by Christians who want to assert that the reality behind the outmoded language remains unchanged. Those persons who are tempted to think that the whole business is just a matter of finding the right word ought to recall that Gabriel Vahanian (who in some ways began everything with a book titled *The Death of God,* back in 1961) reminds us of the problem with easy solution. "All of us," he said, ". . . would do well to ponder the experience of translating the Latin Mass into the vernacular only to discover that it became even more meaningless."[6] There is no doubt that much of what we say is unnecessarily obscured by the comfortable words of our habits and traditions, but that is not adequate to bear the weight of the claim that God is dead.

It might even be, Altizer and Hamilton suggested, that the Christian story no longer possesses the power to capture and heal. It may be that the concepts of God as problem solver, absolute power, necessary being, ultimate concern are inadequate or even destructive. (One hears Dietrich Bonhoeffer again, in this proposal. He thought the God of classical metaphysics, the God who complemented and fulfilled "religious" people in their largely concocted weaknesses, the God who stepped into the otherwise insoluble puzzles of our life—the "gaps" of life—was entirely inappropriate.)

And although Hamilton has done as much talking about the hidden God as anyone, together he and Altizer seem to suggest that the death of God is not a passing human experience that will, if we are patient and faithful, go away. Nor are they simply arguing, in a kind of Barthian way, that we have simply gone whoring after false gods again, who deserve to die. Neither is it just that God has to die "out there" in the world so that he can find life in us. The death of God is not mysticism.

Even the curious bystander soon discovers that the death of God is very nearly all things to all men. There is no death-of-God school, no required curriculum, no faculty. Gabriel Vahanian denies what he very early described. Everyone agrees that William Hamilton and Thomas Altizer are talking about the death of God, although they almost seem to be describing two different events. Paul van Buren is often called a death-of-God theologian, although he protests his inclusion, suggesting that the term is linguistically absurd. Richard Rubenstein, a Jew who has written some of the most powerful material on the subject, says that the title is so identifiably Christian that he is uneasy with the label. As has already been suggested, Dietrich Bonhoeffer began something—something unfinished—as he tried to work Karl Barth out of his system and the world back into it. Paul Tillich, as incurably ontological as he was (apologies to Bonhoeffer), belongs here. And the father of them all, Friedrich Nietzsche (apologies to Richard Rubenstein), who warned us he was a hundred years too early, towers over them all.

I do not propose to review all these good gentlemen, or even adequately to report on a selected few of them. But if the God problem today has two legs, surely one of them is the assertion that God is dead. What I *will* do is point out some of the claims of some of those reporters of God's demise. (Nietzsche demands more credit than that: he not only reported, he *willed* God's death. Altizer thinks that it is a good idea, too. Hamilton rejoices; Rubenstein grieves.) I shall begin in the middle, I think, with Dietrich Bonhoeffer, although I haven't the faintest idea what he is the middle of. He, arrested by the Nazis for plotting to assassinate Hitler, wrote the most startling things while he waited to be hanged.

DIETRICH BONHOEFFER

Dietrich Bonhoeffer wrote to his friend Eberhard Bethge:

You would be surprised, and perhaps even worried, by my theological thoughts and the conclusions that they lead to. . . . What is bothering me incessantly is the question of what Christianity really is, or indeed who Christ really is, for us today. . . . We are moving towards a completely religionless time; people as they are now simply cannot be religious any more.[7]

To appreciate Bonhoeffer's talk about "religionless Christianity," it is necessary to understand something of the way he uses the term religion. Like most Western theologians of his generation, Bonhoeffer was reared on a generous diet of neo-orthodox theology. He was one of a generation of Christians shaped by Karl Barth, which is also to say that he was a grandchild of nineteenth-century liberal theology. Neo-orthodox theologians, mirroring Barth's own experience, were a reaction against what seemed to them to be an unholy optimism about human possibilities. Barth afterward referred to the time of the generation of men before him as "the good old days" and told how one day in August of 1914 the good old days ended. Ninety-three German intellectuals, some of whom had been Barth's fathers in the faith, signed a proclamation in support of the war policy of Kaiser Wilhelm II.[8] According to Barth, the basic error of nineteenth-century theology was its notion that theology had to do with man's possibilities for apprehending God. Ludwig Feuerbach and Friedrich Nietzsche and Adolf von Harnack and Wilhelm Herrmann all lay back there, but it was primarily Friedrich Schleiermacher with whom Barth disputed. Schleiermacher had spoken of religion as the sense of absolute dependence on God and had, from that elementary point, constructed a whole theology that began with man's feelings of dependence. Barth concluded that any religious system that began as Schleiermacher's did, with man and his senses, was certain to end up in something like August of 1914, with no absolute ground from which to judge human perversity. In fact, Barth called every theology that began with the human situation "religion." "Religion" was whatever began with man and aspired to rise to God. In contrast to that, Barth asserted "biblical faith," which as he understood it was the affirmation of the primacy and all-sufficiency of God in his dealings with man. "Biblical faith" was the conviction that salvation lies only in the movement from God toward man. "Faith" began with God and descended to man, particularly in the incarnation. Bonhoeffer's generation learned to use "religion" as the alternative to "faith." "Religion" was ego, pride, futility, self-justification. God was holy, wholly other: man the recipient of saving action. The understanding of man that resulted from neo-orthodox theology was negative. The action belonged to God, and God acted to forgive the sinner, whose proper response was gratitude.

Bonhoeffer stood that business on its head. The notion that man was as futile and hopeless as Barth had said offended him. "Religious people," Bonhoeffer said, "speak of God when human knowledge (perhaps simply because they are too lazy to think) has come to an end or when human resources fail. . . ."[9] It seemed to Bonhoeffer that "religion," understood that way, was what people were like when they were pressed to their limits and beyond. "Are they to be the chosen few? Is it on this dubious group of people that we are to pounce in fervour, pique, or indignation, in order to sell them our goods?"[10] If they are "religious," and if faith ought to have something to do not only with the extremities of life but with the center of life as well, the question is how Christ can become the Lord of the "religionless" as well. Sometimes Bonhoeffer also used the term religion to refer to the whole world view of such people, their metaphysics and their affirmations of miserable inwardness.

Bonhoeffer had nothing but scorn for those who attempted to make Christians of people by forcing them to accept that helpless view of themselves. Both existentialist philosophy and psychotherapy, he said, took otherwise secure, contented, and happy men and tried to demonstrate to them how really unhappy and miserable they were, so that, properly desperate, they could be rescued from their despair and be made secure, contented, and happy.

Wherever there is health, strength, security, simplicity, they sent luscious fruit to gnaw at or to lay their pernicious eggs in. They set themselves to drive people inward to despair, and then the game is in their hands. That is secularized methodism. And whom does it touch? A small number of intellectuals, of degenerates.[11]

People, Bonhoeffer thought, aren't like that except when driven to extremes. The result is that religion becomes a possibility only at the edges of life, in the weaknesses of life, in the despair of life. Instead:

I should like to speak of God not on the boundaries but at the centre, not in weakness but in strength; and therefore not in death and guilt but in man's life and goodness.[12]

I therefore want to start from the premise that God should not be smuggled into some last secret place, but that we should frankly recognize that the world, and people, have come of age, that we should not run man down in his worldliness, but confront him with

God at his strongest point, that we should give up all our clerical tricks, and not regard psychotherapy and existentialist philosophy as God's pioneers.[13]

In neo-orthodoxy, "religion" was every pretense that man could aspire to God. So fervently was that pretense condemned that every capability of man seemed to be included in the condemnation. And it is the case that neo-orthodoxy, mostly because of its need to deny every shred of nineteenth-century optimism, had a jaundiced view of men. How Dietrich Bonhoeffer, sitting in a prison cell where the Nazis had locked him, ever sensed a new mood of human contentment and competence is a wonder (if not even a miracle)! But he did. Whether he was right or wrong is beside the point. He could not be "religious" any longer, not if being religious meant what neo-orthodox practice had made it to be, not if it meant "what one might call the 'clerical' sniffing-around-after-people's-sins in order to catch them out."[14] He found that to be pointless, ignoble, and unchristian.[15] The problem, then, was how to speak of God without "religion," how to speak in a secular way about God.[16]

For Karl Barth, "religion" was human arrogance toward God, and "faith" was the acceptance, by the grateful sinners, of God-instituted salvation. It seemed to Bonhoeffer that in actual practice neo-orthodox Christianity demanded something like infantile behavior of people, and Bonhoeffer called that attitude of low self-esteem "religion." Bonhoeffer tarred Barth with his own brush.

But what began in *Letters and Papers* as a discussion of religion, or religionless Christianity, very quickly became a discussion about God. To be "religious," as Bonhoeffer saw it, was to believe that a person was closest to important things at the extremities of life. Man in despair, man in recognition of his essential helplessness, was ready for God. The consequence was that God came to be regarded as a stopgap for extreme situations. Ordinary, healthy people didn't need God —not that kind of God.

Man has learnt to deal with himself in all questions of importance without recourse to the "working hypothesis" called "God." . . .

It is becoming evident that everything gets along without "God"—and, in fact, just as well as before. . . . "God" is being pushed more and more out of life, losing more and more ground.[17]

Faced with such common, competent people (the world is full of them), the church laid those pernicious eggs of doubt and despair and tried to convince a world thus come of age that it needed rescue, salvation, health, and tutelage: "God." "God," wrote Bonhoeffer, "is no stop-gap; he must be recognized at the centre of life, not when we are at the end of our resources."[18] When God was displaced from common ("secular") life, the attempt was made to secure a refuge for him in the sphere of the personal, the inner, and the private. "The secrets known to a man's valet—that is, to put it crudely, the range of his intimate life, from prayer to his sexual life—have become the hunting ground of modern pastoral workers."[19] Bonhoeffer called that "religious blackmail."[20]

It is evident that, just as he rejected "religion," Bonhoeffer also rejected that understanding of the God who acts in response to save religious people, the God in the gaps, or the God who deals with occasional personal disasters. That wasn't God. Bonhoeffer used "God" in two ways, then, and he did not always distinguish them. He said that we have to live in the world as if there were no God, and that is what God demands of us.

God would have us to know that we must live as men who manage our lives without him. The God who is with us is the God who forsakes us. . . . The God who lets us live in the world without the working hypothesis of God is the God before whom we stand continually. Before God and with God we live without God.[21]

Now that is confusing talk! "Before God and with God we live without God." If there are not two definitions of God in there, then Bonhoeffer wrote nonsense.

Bonhoeffer was no atheist. He believed in God, but not a God "out there" or "at the edges" or only "in the gaps." He was really not terribly radical. In effect Bonhoeffer only relocated God from the edges to the center. Or at least he said that is what he *wanted* to do. He tried to do it by denying that what most "religious" people called God was God at all. We can do without that God. *That* God debases man and keeps him in adolescence. But *God*: Bonhoeffer believed in *God*. He was at the center, in the middle of the village, not on the edges. Unfortunately *saying* so does not *make* it so. Bonhoeffer himself admitted that in the center of ordinary human life there was no need for God, no apprehension of him, no detectable place for him: "everything gets along without God." But it is precisely *there* that Bonhoeffer tried to find God. There is no evidence that he succeeded, in spite of saying so. It is tiresome and true that Bonhoeffer did not leave us a finished theology. Much of the lamenting over that fact is focused on the dilemma of perceiving what "God in the middle of things" means. "Perhaps if Bonhoeffer had lived. . . ." One might indeed wait for the other shoe to drop, but it will not be *that* shoe. It is infinitely harder to affirm God in the middle than at the edges, and it is hopeless at the edges. Changing God's geography is no solution at all. Bonhoeffer was right about a lot of things, but he was wrong about the relocation of God. God isn't *there* either.

The ambiguity of Bonhoeffer's language about God is evident in some of the work of the death-of-God theologians, particularly in William Hamilton's earlier writings. Hamilton also distinguished between two Gods in his 1961 book, *The New Essence of Christianity*. He called one the God of the Augustinian-Reformed tradition, the remote, sovereign, and omnipotent God who is not only far from us but who has departed from us. "It is a very short step, but a critical one, to move from the otherness of God to the absence of God."[22]

The God seen as a person, making the world, manipulating some people towards good, condemning other people to damnation—the objectified God, in other words—this is the God many have declared to be dead today. This is the God who must disappear, so that we may remake our thinking and our speaking about him.[23]

It is what Hamilton calls "the traditional God" who has died. And in his place Hamilton thinks "the impotent God, suffering with men, seems to be emerging."[24] But it is plain that to put the death of God in those terms is not to speak of God at all but to speak of our conceptions of God, and sometimes Hamilton says it that way: "when we speak of the death of God, we speak not only of the death of idols or the falsely objectified being in one sky; we speak, as well, of the death in us of any power to affirm any of the traditional images of God."[25] Those are statements about us, not about God: "the death *in us* of . . . traditional *images of God*."

PAUL TILLICH

I have already suggested a few of the ways in which contemporary discussions about God are in debt (and in reaction) to Karl Barth and Dietrich Bonhoeffer. A considerable debt is also owed to Paul Tillich, whose talk about God was always provocative. Tillich was always quick to distinguish between a theistic conception of God (God as a person of some kind) and a God somehow beyond that. One sees in Hamilton the same kind of distinction, although the language has shifted considerably.

Tillich was always amazed by the hostile reactions he got to a short discussion about God at the end of his book, *The Courage to Be.*[26] In that discussion of the kind of courage it takes to find meaning in the face of so much evident meaninglessness, Tillich referred to the "God above God" or to "God beyond God." Here again, as with both Bonhoeffer and Hamilton, the term God is used in two senses. The God who is to be surpassed, as Tillich explained it, is the God of theism. Theism, he said, can mean any of three things. (Tillich had a category for everything: everything in the system; a system for everything. When Tillich finished explaining what his opponents meant in terms of his own system, they always felt as if they had been cordially received in the wrong house; the slippers and smoking jacket were the right size but belonged to someone else.)

Some people use "God" to create a reverent mood, or to get elected to public office, or because they really cannot understand what the world would be without a god. Sometimes "God" is a way of talking about ethical ideals or emotional states (although I do not see how the latter two uses are necessarily theistic). It is against this first wooly kind of theism that much atheism is directed, and the atheism is as nebulous as the theism it denies. That theism, Tillich says, is irrelevant.

Some theists call themselves theists because the term enables them to talk about a "face to face" experience they wish to affirm. This second kind of theism focuses on personalistic biblical passages, anthropomorphic images of God, the personal nature of faith and forgiveness, the conflict between God's holiness and man's sinfulness, and the intimate and reciprocal nature of prayer. This kind of theism, Tillich thought, was one-sided.

Worse than either of those is the belief in God as a being alongside of, and like, other beings. God as *a* being may be said to be the most important, powerful, gracious, and marvelous of all beings, but however he is described, he is still just one part of reality, subject to the limitations of all being. "He is seen as a self which has a world, as an ego which is related to a thou, as a cause which is separated from its effect, as having a definite space and an endless time. He is a being, not being-itself."[27] God, conceived of that way, is a part of all subject-object reality. We see God as an object, and God as subject objectifies us. "He deprives me of my subjectivity because he is all-powerful and all-knowing."[28] It is an unequal match and, Tillich says, God appears as the invincible tyrant. He becomes the model of everything against which existentialism revolted. That kind of God becomes personally responsible for the injustices of his world. There lies the deepest root of atheism, Tillich thought: "This is the God Nietzsche said had to be killed because nobody can tolerate being made into a mere object of absolute knowledge and absolute control."[29]

I don't find those categories of theism to be terribly self-evident or instructive, but over against all of them (but particularly the last) Tillich spoke of the other God: one might say the God beyond theism or above theism. "Theism," he said, ". . . is transcended in the experience we have called absolute faith."[30] (Tillich spoke easily about absolutes, which is one of the ways in which he was not a contemporary man.) The Reformation doctrine of justification by grace through faith is, in Tillich's terminology, a matter of accepting the fact of being accepted. It is not an aggressive self-justification; it is acceptance of our own acceptability, a gift, a being grasped.

The theist will say that it is "God" who accepts us. Tillich tries to go "beyond" ("above") that: absolute faith "is the accepting of the acceptance *without somebody or something that accepts.* It is the power of being-itself that accepts and gives the courage to be. . . . The ultimate source of the courage to be is the 'God above God.' "[31] (Italics added.) It is the power of being that grasps us, the ground of being.

Because ontology was his basic category, everything for Tillich came out in terms of being, and if God were not a being alongside other beings (in effect making God just another creature, however remarkable a one), then God had to be that which made finite being possible: hence, God the ground of being or power of being. Tillich talked about being-itself as if it were something, a thing that stretched, reached out, took form, and resisted nonbeing. It is a peculiar way to talk, and he had to invent ways to explain what he meant. That "God above God" was more personal than persons, acted not like other actors but was *in* every act, more real than any finite being, and (note this!) "is present, although hidden, in every divine-human encounter."[32] (Decency *demands* that God be present in every divine-human encounter.) Whereas theists speak of the one who forgives guilt, for the nontheist no person or alien power acts on us. "The Lutheran courage returns but not supported by the faith in a judging and forgiving God. It returns in terms of the absolute faith which says Yes although there is no special power that conquers guilt."[33] Courage to be in the face of meaninglessness is reestablished in the power of God above the God of theism, the courage to take meaninglessness upon oneself. *"The courage to be is rooted in the God who appears when God has disappeared in the anxiety of doubt."*[34]

All through the early stages of the death-of-God theology one finds this Tillichian kind of God-language, not so much an acceptance of his ontological categories as it is a denial of the "God" who has become an embarrassment and an affirmation and anticipation of the real God. The problem is that the God above God is a lot less believable than the deity he replaces. "Being-itself," or "the ground of being," isn't something or someone (as Tillich insists), but *what* it is is more of a mystery than an explanation. The difference between God above God and no God at all is not clear except to the person who can, as Tillich did, think of being almost as if it were something. It isn't. It is an abstraction, and abstractions do not "accept" people. Perhaps it is the case that God, as Tillich prefers to think of God, is a peculiar but important way to say something about personal courage or self-affirmation or, as Nietzsche might have put it, of the will to power.

WILLIAM HAMILTON

What is evident in all the men we have been discussing is the common determination to reject an inadequate or unworthy idea of God. Barth rejected the God of "religion" for the God of faith, Bonhoeffer used the same language but changed the content, Tillich affirmed a "God above God," and Hamilton rejected the traditional Augustinian-Reformed portrait of God. However one says it, the contemporary experience is that *God,* as God has been generally understood, is unbelievable. One can see that determination to think differently about God in "the early Hamilton," too. Indirectly responding to a Philip Toynbee suggestion that what we can do is simply wait for God and focus our energies on specific and personal rather than vaguely general activities, Hamilton said, "Waiting here refers to the whole experience I have called 'the death of God,' including the attack on religion and the search for a means by which God, not needed, may be enjoyed."[35] Bonhoeffer had rejected any notion of God whose function it was to "save" man from life's boundary situations. God wasn't the answer to man's unsolved problems. That is the language of personal salvation, and Bonhoeffer thought that questions of salvation were characteristic neither of contemporary man nor the biblical materials. Particularly in his earlier articles, Hamilton reflected that same attitude.

To assert that we are men moving from cloister to world, church to world, to say that we are secular men, is to say that we do not ask God to do for us what the world is qualified to do. Really to travel along this road means that we trust the world, not God, to be our need fulfiller and problem solver, and God, if he is to be for us at all, must come in some other role.[36]

Hamilton may have rejected the God of the Augustinian-Reformed tradition with his left hand, but he welcomed another Calvinistic God with his right: God, they both say, is to be delighted in forever. "If God is not needed, if it is to the world and not God that we repair for our needs and problems, then perhaps we may come to see that he is to be enjoyed and delighted in."[37] There is a faint odor of desperation in this kind of talk about God. A God that is unrelated to all the ordinary problems and possibilities of life is a peculiar God to be delighting in. For what reason? God as a house cat! "Our waiting for God, our godlessness, is partly a search for a language and a style by which we might be enabled to stand before him once again, delighting in his presence."[38] That is pretty insubstantial stuff, and it is probably no surprise that the death-of-God theologians soon abandoned that way of talking. It is important, though, because it so clearly reveals what is a very common human experience regarding God, and the sense of loss and lack of meaning that the name conveys. In Hamilton's early theology, the desire at least to delight in God, who in all other ways did not make sense, is closely related to the hope that, false Gods having been denied, the real God will finally appear. Hamilton waited for that God. The death of God, in that sense, was a "death in us of any power to affirm any of the traditional images of God."[39] That, he said, was the special Christian burden of our time, the situation of being without. "There is, for some reason, no possession of God for us, but only a hope, only a waiting."[40]

"The absent one has a kind of presence."[41] Perhaps that is the heart of Hamilton's enduring optimism. It may be the case that Hamilton isn't waiting anymore. Perhaps waiting is too much the product of a Barthian distinction between the gods of religion and the God of genuine faith, those who deserve to die and the one who lives forever. If the evident optimistic tone of Hamilton's work is not the consequence of a God somewhere in the works, then it must be based on an underlying positive assessment of the possibilities for man. One of his articles is titled "The New Optimism—From Prufrock to Ringo."[42] I suspect one of the reasons neo-orthodoxy doesn't convince any longer is that this pessimism doesn't persuade any more.[43] Hamilton has subsequently explained that opti-

mism may be too naïve a term, but still he affirms a sense in which our time has genuine possibilities for human action, for human happiness, for human decency. That is a curious affirmation, since in the *New Essence* Hamilton had cited the insanity of suffering in the world as one of the reasons why belief in God (*that* God?) was impossible. Rieux in Camus' *The Plague* said to the priest, upon realizing that they *were* allies against death and disease, although not agreed on God's role in it, "God himself can't part us now." Later Hamilton thought that the death of God was precisely the reason for optimism: "The death of tragedy is due to the death of God."[44] It is hard to know whether the ace up Hamilton's sleeve is a better God or a better man. Without one or the other, the optimism is foolishness. In that respect he is very different from Richard Rubenstein, whose assessment of our situation is bleaker than Hamilton's. Whether Hamilton has abandoned his wait for a return of God or not, and he seems to say he has, although what that abandonment means in the light of his own good humor about the matter is puzzling, what he does embody is a common sense of the loss of God, "in *our* time, in *our* history, in *our* existence," as Altizer put it, or, to quote Hamilton, "There really is a sense of not-having, of not-believing, of having lost, not just the idols or the gods of religion, but God himself. And this is an experience that is not peculiar to a neurotic few, nor is it private or inward. Death of God is a public event in our history."[45]

When William Hamilton says God died, he does not really mean God died. When he first said it he seemed to have meant that God went away, or some such thing, and we miss him. It is hard to know whether Hamilton still thinks God is playing cat and mouse, or whether he thinks that belief in God, once possible, is neither possible nor desirable any longer. In any event, the focus of his attention is on what that means for man. He seems to prefer not to talk about God.

THOMAS ALTIZER

Thomas Altizer, in contrast, is talking about *God*. When he says God died, he means *God* did something. "God is not simply hidden from view, nor is he lurking in the depths of our unconscious or on the boundaries of our infinite space, nor

will he appear on the next turn of an historical wheel of fate."[46] The death of God, as Altizer explains it, is culturally apprehended and does have social and cultural consequences. But it is not just a name for something that people feel, nor is it just a description of the difficulty of faith such as we have inherited it. It is all that, but it is not just that. In fact, at the center it is primarily a metaphysical event, but a metaphysical event that involves physical reality in its performance. "There is . . . no escaping the inevitable consequence that the dead God is not the God of idolatry, or false piety, or 'religion,' but rather the God of the historic Christian Church, and beyond the Church, of Christendom at large."[47] The God who died actually did live, in the past, distinct from man and the world, but now *that* God is dead.

Altizer believes that *God* died, but not that God *died*. God, as a transcendent being, the God of Abraham and Isaac and Jacob, the God who really was there, is no longer there. The whole realm of the transcendent has collapsed, and we know it. We feel it, and the sense of emptiness is profound and genuine. God *that way* is no longer there, and that is what Altizer calls death of God. But death is not really a good word for what he means. Altizer is a Hegelian, and he believes that we are caught up in a gigantic and profound process in which something is happening to the whole of reality. God, as he was, is no more. God invested himself in Jesus in the incarnation, and in the crucifixion of Jesus that transcendent God "died." It might be more accurate to say that the assuming of flesh—the incarnation itself—was the death of the transcendent God. The resurrection of Christ (Jesus died; Christ was resurrected) is the appearance of God in a new form in the world. The transcendent God has become immanent. The world of the spirit poured itself into the world and became flesh. So, Altizer says, "faith must come to know the death of God as an historical event witnessing to the advent of a new form of the Word. . . . Only a new Adam who is liberated from the old creation of the past can celebrate the presence of the Word in a new world that negates all previous forms of faith."[48]

To know the death of God is not easy. It is to live in darkness or, as Altizer otherwise expresses it, to "wager" every-

thing. But God's "death" is necessary, and the Christian must not only accept it but *will* it. "If theology is truly to die, it must *will* the death of God, must *will* the death of Christendom, must freely choose the destiny before it, and therefore must cease to be itself."[49] (Theology and Christendom here refer to that thought and life appropriate to God as a transcendent being.) Or to put it even more strongly, "It is the Christian who must murder God, or, rather, it is the Christian who must bury the decomposing God who continues to haunt our memory of things past."[50] If the incarnation, the death of God, is the descent of God into human flesh, then we can no longer speak of an exalted Lord or a cosmic Logos. The forms that the sacred took in the past must be rejected. "Only a theology which abandons an original and primordial sacred, and opens itself to a forward moving process of repetition, can acknowledge that God has truly and actually become incarnate in concrete space and time."[51]

As a consequence of his clearly unusual conception of the incarnation, Altizer has only incidental continuing interest in the historical Jesus. The Jesus of whom we learn in the Gospels is inseparable from precisely those models of thought that have become not only impossible but destructive for us. "Increasingly there is the recognition that to the extent that we imagine Jesus in his traditional Christian form we are closed to his contemporary presence."[52]

Christ is present for us: God in his new form. God died in Jesus, or with Jesus, and that death is now being realized in contemporary culture. As another writer puts it, "It means the death of the traditional God of transcendence and the birth of a new Christ of radical immanence."[53] In *The Gospel of Christian Atheism*, Altizer called the business of turning away from the transcendent phase to God now present in Christ a kind of wager:

Dare we bet that the Christian God is dead, that the ultimate ground of guilt and resentment is broken, and that our guilty condition is created by our clinging to the wholly alien power of a now emptied transcendent realm? . . . When the Christian bets that God is dead, he is betting upon the real and actual presence of the fully incarnate Christ. Thus a Christian wager upon the death of God is a wager upon the presence of the living Christ, a bet that Christ is now at least potentially present in a new and total form.[54]

Christ will not become clearly present to us until we have died to every vestige of his transcendent image. So Altizer would hurl us into an absolute immanence.

"It is my persuasion," Altizer said, "that the thinker who has most truly understood the revolutionary and dialectical meaning of faith is Hegel, and that we must ever return to Hegel for a theoretical understanding of the meaning of a movement of dialectical negation."[55] The death of God, as Altizer professes it, is the Hegelian self-annihilation of the spirit, pouring itself into the world and becoming flesh. The present stage is itself preliminary to a final eschatological stage in which God will be all in all, in which the distinction between God and man will be completely merged. First the incarnate Word "empties itself of Spirit so as to appear and exist as flesh," and the Christian "must finally look forward to the resurrection of the profane in a transfigured and thus finally sacred form."[56]

Altizer's commitment to a Hegelian vision of the movement of history causes him to seek for the reconciliation of seemingly hopeless opposites into something new. He believes that by affirming the death of God, God will be enabled to live in new form, that the divine and the human will find new unity, that only the radically profane can witness to the movement of the sacred. Paradox is the only adequate language for him.

As Kierkegaard saw so deeply, faith in the Incarnation is faith in the truly absurd. Therefore the only adequate language for the Incarnation is the language of paradox, of the deepest paradox, which may well mean that it is only the language of the radically profane that can give witness to the fullest advent of the Incarnation. When faith is open to the most terrible darkness, it will be receptive to the most redemptive light. What can the Christian fear of darkness, when he knows that Christ has conquered darkness, that God will be all in all?[57]

So, again, the Christian must *will* the death of God, in order that, by affirming the profanity of the Incarnation as death, the holy and the profane may move toward the end of history when they together become something radically new.

It is evident now that Altizer is *not* a secular theologian. At the most profound level he is talking about God and the manner in which the sacred is moving toward consummation with matter. The *transcendent* God no longer exists for Altizer— he is dead—but that loss is necessary for a fuller realization of the sacred. It will be lamented—in a sense, it must be lamented—but at the deepest level that is not a *loss* of God, only of a former manifestation of God. To the extent that William Hamilton, Harvey Cox, or Paul van Buren are secular, Altizer must be distinguished from them. The death of God for Altizer is really part of a fuller revelation of God. He is profoundly an affirmer of the reality of God. Everything is moving toward an eschatological realization of God as all in all.

Dietrich Bonhoeffer, for all his talk about being without God, really only relocated God from the periphery to the center. William Hamilton is either still waiting for God or he ignores God, as if all that talk about God were not about *something*. And Thomas Altizer is anything *but* a secular man, however much the language of dialectic allows him to play hide-and-seek games with the sacred and the profane. Altizer has a God, a Hegelian God, who is subject to a process that is larger than God himself. Altizer even knows what God eventually will become. That is remarkable knowledge. Altizer's God has a God, too, and Hegel has described him best. In fact, Hegel created him.

It is strange business to read Altizer's theology. He reports the activities and intentions of a process that seems to stand over us. There is a world of reality out there that ordinary people simply cannot see and scarcely can believe. Bonhoeffer found that a God out there somewhere was impossible for contemporary men to understand, and he asserted (without any evidence of it) that God wasn't out there at all: God was in here, precisely where Bonhoeffer himself admitted we had no cause at all to speak of a divine presence. Altizer tries to repeat the same trick. He, too, found transcendent divinity too much for credulity. So he moved God closer to things than things are to themselves. But what reason have we to believe that? Altizer's theological system is almost the epitome of what it is contemporary men *cannot* understand. In that respect he shares a great deal with the whole process school of theology. They, even more than Altizer, still have another reality out there somewhere, whose name is God. They have tried to invest God with relativity and development and to abandon the language of absolutes, and that is a good thing. Altizer, like process theology, still does not face the long, powerful, increasingly compelling recognition that there is just one reality: this one. Moving God in here with us, hiding him nearby, will not do. In that respect, Richard Rubenstein has looked deeper into the darkness.

RICHARD RUBENSTEIN

There is no dancing at the death of God for Richard Rubenstein. William Hamilton has said that he is "more inclined to think of celebration, and of comedy," than of requiems; that "the death of God is not a sorrowful death really."[58] Nietzsche's Zarathustra said that he should only believe in a God that would know how to dance,[59] and it is clear that neither Nietzsche nor Rubenstein thinks God ever learned.

In the forward to Elie Wiesel's book *Night*, François Mauriac described the young man who had lived through the holocaust, who lived to write *Night*, and to tell of the hanging of another child:

For him Nietzsche's cry expressed an almost physical reality: God is dead, the God of love, of gentleness, of comfort, the God of Abraham, of Isaac, of Jacob, has vanished forevermore, beneath the gaze of this child, in the smoke of a human holocaust exacted by Race, the most voracious of all idols. And how many pious Jews have experienced this death! On that day, horrible even among those days of horror, when the child watched the hanging (yes!) of another child, who, he tells us, had the face of a sad angel, he heard someone behind him groan: "Where is God? Where is He? Where can He be now?" and a voice within me answered: "Where? Here He is—He has been hanged here, on these gallows."[60]

Richard Rubenstein told how, in his experience, the fact of the prison camps pressed in on his own life. In 1961 he went to Germany, precisely at the time of the closing of the border between East and West Berlin. The occasion prompted several discussions, one of which was with a prominent Protestant church official in Berlin. Dean Heinrich Grüber (who later protested that he was misunderstood or misquoted) apparently maintained that even the incarceration and liquidation of six million Jews under Hitler had to be understood as the will of God. At least, Rubenstein understood Grüber to be arguing that if God were the omnipotent author of the historical drama, and if Israel were his chosen people, then God was in some way responsible for Israel's devastation. Whether or not Grüber and Rubenstein agreed on the precise course of their conversation, Rubenstein concluded that something was wrong with the theology of both of them when a decent human being like the Dean could speak (as any traditional Christian or Jewish theologian might legitimately have done) of God's Lordship over the death camps.[61]

Over and over again Rubenstein asserts that the experience of Jews during World War II marks a tragic point of no return for Jewish theology. "Although Jewish history is replete with disaster, none has been so radical in its total import as the holocaust. Our images of God, man, and the moral order have been permanently impaired."[62] It is, he says, *the* question that all Jewish theology must deal with if it is to have the slightest relevance to contemporary Jewish life. For that reason he expresses amazement that traditional Jewish theology *does* continue. It is traditional Jewish (and Christian) theology to maintain that God is the ultimate, omnipotent actor in the historical drama, and that theology has interpreted every major catastrophe in Jewish history as God's punishment for sinful Israel. Rubenstein does not see how that concept of God can be maintained *without* calling him the Lord of the death camps and without regarding Hitler and the SS as instruments of God's will. "The idea is simply too obscene for me to accept."[63] With Wiesel, Rubenstein says, "God really died at Auschwitz."[64] "If there were such a God, the death camps were ultimately his handiwork. This idea places too great a strain on our credulity. Our death-of-God experience rests on a loss of faith in the God-who-acts-in-history."[65] Rubenstein finds Karl Barth's dramatic separation of the ways of God from the ways of man a consequence of recognizing such impossibilities in traditional belief in God. Rubenstein occasionally cites other reasons for finding something like a death-of-God experience inescapable, but it is clear that because he is a Jew, it is the holocaust first of all that arrests him. In that respect he is very unlike Hamilton and Altizer, whose theologies are not born in tragedy. "All Jews (and Christians, though it is less obvious with them) are at least two thousand years old the day they are born."[66] Theology that is born in ovens cannot be the same as theology born in less ghastly places. Rather than celebration, comedy, or joy, as seems to be the case for Altizer and Hamilton, Rubenstein is saddened by the death of God, finding no reason to dance at the funeral: "If I am a death of God theologian, it is with a cry of agony."[67] "We shall learn bitterly to regret our loss of innocence."[68]

"I believe," Rubenstein said, "that the death of God is a cultural event. It has been experienced by millions of men and women who have had to face the collapse of religious faith and authority."[69] When he said that, Rubenstein seemed to want to distinguish himself from Altizer, who, he said, maintained that God literally died in our times. Whether or not it is appropriate to say Altizer thinks God "literally" died, it is plain they mean two different things. By calling the death of God a cultural event, Rubenstein seems to mean at least two things. First, the experience is not common only to a few people. Millions of men and women know it. And second, the death of God is a realization of something that has always been so, but about which we were mistaken. It is, as already mentioned, a loss of innocence. The term is significant, Rubenstein says, in what it reveals about those who assert it. The death of God is information concerning what we believe about God, not about God. God, he says, is totally unavailable to us as a source of meaning or value. Rubenstein said:

When I say we live in the time of the death of God, I mean that the thread uniting God and man, heaven and earth, has been broken. We stand in a cold, silent, unfeeling cosmos, unaided by any purposeful power beyond our own resources. After Auschwitz, what else can a Jew say about God?[70]

We were mistaken. That is clear, now.

Rubenstein rejects theism. "A God who tolerates the suffering of even one innocent child is either infinitely cruel or hopelessly indifferent."[71] Our fathers, recognizing that problem, needed the projection of another future existence to rectify the injustices of this life. In itself, he writes, that is an implicit criticism of God's government. "I do not believe," he asserts, "that a theistic God is necessary for Jewish religious life."[72] He might more accurately have said "possible" rather than necessary. The transcendent Father-God is dead, not in the way that Altizer describes it, as a change from one state of being to another, but dead in the sense that the whole concept is inadequate and probably has been so for a long while. "One cannot pray to such a God in the hope of achieving an I-Thou relationship. Such a God is not a person over against man."[73]

There are other reasons for rejecting the idea of God as a person who confronts us as lesser persons. In *The Courage to Be*, as we saw earlier, Tillich said that God had to be something above or beyond theism. Rubenstein, whose earlier work, particularly, showed evidence of considerable Tillichian influence, agreed with Tillich that a theistic God who manipulates the cosmos ultimately stands as the enemy of human freedom: "human moral autonomy is incompatible with the traditional conception of a personal God."[74] Rubenstein and Altizer are agreed that Paul Tillich's influence on contemporary theology is profound. Rubenstein, in a 1955 essay, used Tillich's "ground of being" language to describe God and described human existence as a kind of standing out from being itself, quite as Tillich himself did. He even uses the definition of God as the focus of ultimate concern,[75] but it seems fair to say in most of his subsequent writing Rubenstein intends something more radical than Tillich's terminology and ontological categories permit. But he has not completely abandoned the images Tillich might use. In *Morality and Eros* he described human life as a kind of wave that stands out from the ocean of being, seeking to find its own being, an ultimately impossible attempt. He does caution, though, that the image is a metaphor and ought not to be pressed too far.

None of the other theologians whom we have investigated takes so clear and hard-eyed a look at the human situation as Rubenstein does. His honesty is incredible. His evaluation is also strained by his indelible knowledge of the holocaust, but perhaps one ought not to pass Auschwitz unnoticed on one's way to joyful and even comic places. Rubenstein stands at least as a corrective, if not an alternative, to those too easily asserted enthusiasms that Altizer, and particularly Hamilton, declare. Altizer has a reason: he believes God is closer than ever. Hamilton gives the impression, at least, that he has not discovered how large and deep are some of the dark places in man and nature. It is probably also the case, to be fair, that Rubenstein's own vision is *too* much filled with black places. Auschwitz is not *all* that is to be said, either, but it is there, and no Jew ought to let other men forget it. Rubenstein says that in the death of God we have lost our innocence and our comfort, and that is a sorrow. The cosmos, he says, is ultimately absurd and tragic. It is absurd and tragic because human existence is ultimately hopeless and without meaning.[76] The transcendent God is simply gone. There is no Father-God to care. He died at Auschwitz. "We are alone in a silent, unfeeling cosmos. Our actions are human actions. Their entailments are human entailments. . . . Though most of us will refrain from antisocial behavior, we do so because of the fear of ourselves and others rather than fear of God."[77] Rubenstein quotes Zalman Schacter: "If there is a God, He doesn't exist."[78] Rubenstein calls creation a catastrophe. Creatures are caught between trying to be something—a life of tension—and the tendency to slip back into the primordial ground out of which they stand (Tillich again). "We are born but to perish. We are more than the fools of the gods; we are their food."[79] Human existence without a traditional God cannot be based on any hope which transcends the physical man and the time that he has in which to live. "There seems to be little convincing evidence of a redemptive goal or of the notion that man has any special cosmic significance beyond the significance he creates for himself."[80] In that respect Rubenstein sounds quite like Jacques Monod: "The ancient covenant is in pieces; man knows at last that he is alone in the universe's unfeeling immensity, out of which he emerged only by chance."[81] Rubenstein again:

Death is the price we pay for life, love, and joy; so too is our unredeemed existence. This does not mean that we should seek speedily to be redeemed by the awesome angel [death]. On the contrary, we must forsake the quest for redemption and accept life with its limitations and ironies. It is better that the Messiah [death, again] tarry. His kingdom is not of this world. All we have is this world. Let us endure its wounds and celebrate its joys in undeceived lucidity.[82]

Rubenstein does have a God. The office is not vacant. It is filled with as terrible and perplexing a God as one might imagine the holocaust might spare. "The time of the death of God does not mean the end of all gods. It means the demise of the God who was the ultimate actor in history. I believe in God, the Holy Nothingness known to mystics of all ages, out of which we have come and to which we shall ultimately return."[83] On one level, Rubenstein's language about God is terribly puzzling. He intends that, I think. God, as he approves of the term, is not a name for a void. God is the richness from which all existence derives and to which it returns. Rubenstein deliberately uses the ancient practice of referring to God in negatives, on the ground that definitions are appropriate only for finite things. God isn't finite and definable. "The infinite God is nothing."[84] God is the abyss out of which we come. It is important to recognize that as Rubenstein speaks of God, he really intends to say something about man: "Contemporary theology reveals less about God than it does about the kind of men we are. It is largely an anthropological discipline."[85] Death may indeed be the end to pain, greed, and suffering, but it is also an end to the individual identity. To have been created out of Holy Nothingness, and to return to it, is to cease to be someone. "In speaking of God, we formulate an explicit judgment concerning the nature and the limitations of the human condition."[86]

Terms like "Holy Nothingness" or Tillich's use of "ground of being," seem preferable to the biblical image of a Father-

God, according to Rubenstein. He prefers maternal to paternal metaphors. Man is not created, as the biblical imagery suggests, out of something else, but out of God's own substance.[87] That does not mean that God is death. To say that death is a return to Holy Nothingness is to assert plainly that separate human identity ends: "We really know in a total, certain, and non-reasoning way that death entails the final disappearance of the self, the return to Nothingness."[88] But God is the source not just of death but of life, too. Death is the price for life, and they come together. *"Above all, we must not refuse to pay the full price of admission to authentic human existence.* To acknowledge the finality of death requires a certain clarity and a certain courage. God creates out of his own substance. God nurtures, but God also annihilates."[89] In that sense, there is a demonic aspect to reality and to God. *"To say that God and nature are at one with each other, that they are alive and life-engendering, is to affirm the demonic side not alone in us but in divinity as well."*[90]

It is the Messiah who takes us from life to death, who is himself death. Rubenstein cites the novel *The Family Moskat*, in which a Jewish family meets while the Germans are at the gates of Warsaw. One member of the family thinks the Messiah will come quickly. The others are astonished. Hertz Yanovar explains, "Death is the Messiah." Rubenstein says:

The insight is irrefutable. The Messiah traditionally promises an end to the inescapable infirmities and limitations of the human condition. But there is only one way out of the ironies and the dilemmas of existence; that exit is death. . . . This is the only world we shall ever know. Our pleasures must be precious in our sight, for we purchase them with our lives. The Messiah will come. He tarrieth not. We need not welcome Him. The world is not large enough for both mankind and its Redeemer.[91]

Life is bittersweet for Richard Rubenstein.

Dietrich Bonhoeffer had wondered how to think about God without religion. Rubenstein, on the other hand, wonders how to be religious in a time of the death of God. It is precisely in a time like ours that men *need* religion. Now, more than ever, with divine sanctions gone, law, tradition, and structure are necessary for appropriate behavior. Religion, for Rubenstein, is the way men share the predicament of living in an essentially absurd universe that moves from Nothingness to Nothingness, with only the small moments of love and life between. That is something, and something good, but without the community of other men who share this understanding of reality, it would probably be too much to bear. And Judaism? "It is the way we Jews share our lives in an unfeeling and silent cosmos. It is the flickering candle we have lighted in the dark to enlighten and to warm us."[92]

Sometimes Rubenstein does speak as if the empty space where the transcendent God was once imagined to be were filled with a mystical Holy One who is called Nothingness because any other name would make God a something alongside other things. Perhaps that *is* what Rubenstein means. Cox and Bonhoeffer, he said, wanted to speak of God without religion. He himself wants to speak of religion, not without God but in *the time of the death of God*. It may be that Rubenstein's Holy Nothingness is peculiarly something different from the reality that he has created out of himself. It really doesn't matter. Rubenstein also makes it plain that individual human life and consciousness is short and bittersweet. Death is its end. It wouldn't matter, when one's life were irretrievably over, whether what remained was Holy Nothingness or peanut butter. For the *person*, death is the end, and God is not person either. This is almost absolute secularity, with only suspicions of mysticism. Those traces of mysticism are small comfort for anyone trying to salvage even a vestige of future existence.

The term God seems to function for Rubenstein as a term for what precedes man and for what will succeed him. It is a process that produces life and ends it, but which itself is not life or consciousness or person. God, for Rubenstein, seems to be a way of saying that before human life, and after it, there is something, but it is not man, and finally it is inaccessible to us. That is a cold-eyed look at life. It is the first consistent attempt we have seen to be absolutely secular, to pose no reality alongside *this* ordinary reality. It is an attempt to say what God means, but it is finally inadequate, I think. It is almost depressingly pessimistic—a criticism not lightly made in light of the fun-and-games optimism against which Rubenstein reacts. ("Life," a student once told me, "is more than a whorehouse but less than a Christmas tree.") In the second place, God means more than Holy Nothingness. That is simply inadequate to convey the richness of what men have meant when they used the name. And part of the richness of that name has had something to do with delight, and perhaps even play.

It may be that William Hamilton is not playing waiting games with God. If not, then he and Rubenstein are allies in a way that Thomas Altizer cannot share. Altizer is secular only in the most peculiar and misleading sense of the term. He *does* have another reality, if not alongside *this* reality then in the process of merging with it and transforming it into something new. The death of God clearly means different things.

The grandfather of all men to have asserted God's death was Friedrich Nietzsche. There is something to be learned from him.

FRIEDRICH NIETZSCHE

Richard Rubenstein points out that it is awkward for a Jew to use the phrase "death of God" because of the way that designation is grounded in the symbolism of the cross. But "there is no way around Nietzsche."[93] After Nietzsche and after Auschwitz, the vocabulary is fixed for us all; "it is impossible to avoid his language to express the total absence of God from our experience."[94]

Friedrich Nietzsche was born in Prussia in 1844, the son and grandson of Lutheran ministers. History has a curious sense of humor. His father became insane in 1848 and died the following year. Nietzsche and his sister (strange sister) were reared by his mother and three aunts—a five-woman household. (Nietzsche later had unusual opinions about women, none terribly complimentary.) Nietzsche himself became mentally ill and died a virtual vegetable in 1900. It is irresponsible to attribute his opinions to his illness. The body of his work was completed before that happened and, in any case, deserves to be read for what it says. So far as is known, Nietzsche's madness was unrelated to that of his father. Sexually ascetic for most of his life, he did admit to having visited a brothel once or twice as a youth and apparently became mad from tertiary syphilis. He was brilliant, wrote exquisitely, and was appointed to an associate professorship at Basel without having satisfied any of the usual requirements. Neither did he do much of the usual professorial work, and finally the university simply retired him early. After a time he had trouble getting his books published and even more trouble getting them read. He may have been right, as he believed, that he was born a hundred years too early.

Invitation
Venture, comrades, I implore you,
On the fare I set before you,
You will like it more to-morrow,
Better still the following day.[95]

The parable of "The Madman" is the most famous of all of Nietzsche's texts and may still be the best expression of the radical mood in theology:

Have you ever heard of the madman who on a bright morning lighted a lantern and ran to the market-place calling out unceasingly: "I seek God! I seek God!"—As there were many people standing about who did not believe in God, he caused a great deal of amusement. Why! is he lost? said one. Has he strayed away like a child? said another. Or does he keep himself hidden? Is he afraid of us? Has he taken a sea voyage? Has he emigrated?—the people cried out laughingly, all in a hubbub. The insane man jumped into their midst and transfixed them with his glances. "Where is God gone?" he called out. "I mean to tell you! *We have killed him,*—you and I! We are all his murderers! But how have we done it? How were we able to drink up the sea? Who gave us the sponge to wipe away the whole horizon? What did we do when we loosened this earth from its sun? Whither does it now move? Whither do we move? Away from all suns? Do we not dash on unceasingly? Backwards, sideways, forwards, in all directions? Is there still an above and below? Do we not stray, as through infinite nothingness? Does not empty space breathe upon us? Has it not become colder? Does not night come on continually, darker and darker? Shall we not have to light lanterns in the morning?

Do we not hear the noise of the grave-diggers who are burying God? Do we not smell the divine putrefaction?—for even Gods putrefy! God is dead! God remains dead! And we have killed him! How shall we console ourselves, the murderous of all murderers? The holiest and the mightiest that the world has hitherto possessed, has bled to death under our knife,—who will wipe the blood from us? With what water could we cleanse ourselves? What lustrums, what sacred games shall we have to devise? Is not the magnitude of this deed too great for us? Shall we not ourselves have to become Gods, merely to seem worthy of it? There never was a greater event,—and on account of it, all who are born after us belong to a higher history than any history hitherto!"—Here the madman was silent and looked again at his hearers; they also were silent and looked at him in surprise. At last he threw his lantern on the ground, so that it broke in pieces and was extinguished. "I come too early," he then said. "I am not yet at the right time. This prodigious event is still on its way, and is travelling,—it has not yet reached men's ears. Lightning and thunder need time, even after they are done, to be seen and heard. This deed is as yet further from them than the furthest star,—*and yet they have done it!*"— It is further stated that the madman made his way into different churches on the same day, and there intoned his *Requiem aeternam deo.* When led out and called to account, he always gave the reply: "What are these churches now, if they are not the tombs and monuments of God?"[96]

Everything in Nietzsche proceeds from the assumption that God is dead. He doesn't argue about it: he assumes it, and he announces it, and he tries to explain to people who scarcely can believe his words what the consequences of the loss of God mean. Nietzsche called himself an atheist, an unqualified honest atheist. He was that, but his atheism was not simple. His atheism was shaped by a centuries-old Christian culture, and being an atheist in that culture also shaped the nature of his atheism. It was not a narrow negative atheism, a simple nay-saying. Because Nietzsche was comfortable denying God, there is no hysterical shrillness to his charges. *Other* people found it hard to believe that God was dead. In that respect, Nietzsche was a man born out of his time. The announcement of the death of God was only preliminary business for him.

The real questions were what to do, since that was the case. The death-of-God movement of the 1960s is far less sophisticated than Nietzsche in that way. Our own generation found the announcement to be so curious, even exciting, sometimes offensive, that precious little thought has been given to examining what it means in terms of reshaping life and thought. We are still debating whether the whole matter is (or was) just a phase, a smart-alec, shallow digression from the normal theological agenda. Dietrich Bonhoeffer was probably correct when he guessed that the movement toward a secular understanding of the world began in the Middle Ages. One could make a good case that Thomas Aquinas' monumental *Summa* was the last magnificent attempt to hold together the sacred and the secular, nature and grace, the finite and the infinite, time and eternity. Ever since then, particularly since the late seventeenth and eighteenth centuries, the sacred and the secular have grown farther apart, and more and more of common life is transacted without reference to that other reality where God resides. Only when specifically intending to be religious, or on those extreme occasions of disaster or joy, do we resort to the other reality that has shaped all of our talk and thought about God.

Zarathustra, a kind of stand-in for Nietzsche, met an old saint in the forest. The old man had gone into the forest and the desert because he had loved men far too well. Now he loved God; men were far too imperfect. Zarathustra asked the old saint what he did in the forest. The saint answered, "I make hymns and sing them; and in making hymns I laugh and weep and mumble: thus do I praise God." Then the old professional and pious beggar asked what Zarathustra had brought him as a gift. Zarathustra had already said he gave no alms, "I am not poor enough for that." Instead he said that he should hurry away lest he take something away from the old man. They laughed together like schoolboys and parted. When Zarathustra was alone he thought about the divinity he might have robbed from the old man. "Could it be possible!" he said to his heart. "This old saint in the forest hath not yet heard of it, that God is dead!"[97]

With very little evidence for it, Nietzsche did believe that sooner or later—probably later—even Christians would accept the death of God. (That is a courageous hope from a man who had to pay to have much of his work published.) In another passage, Nietzsche described a meeting between Zarathustra and the last pope.

Zarathustra came upon a tall haggard man, dressed in black, looking suspiciously like a priest, seated beside the path. "Another magician," Zarathustra thought, "some sombre wonder-worker of the grace of God, some annointed world-maligner," and wondered how to slip by. But the old man came directly to him. "Whoever thou art, thou traveler," said he, "help a strayed one, a seeker, an old man, who may here easily come to grief!" The old man explained that the world was very strange to him, and remote, and as for the one who could have given him protection, "he is himself no more." He explained he had been seeking the last pious man, a saint and an anchorite, who alone in the forest had not yet heard what the whole world already knew. And *that*? asked Zarathustra: "Perhaps that the old God no longer liveth, in whom all the world once believed?" "Thou sayest it," answered the old man, "and I served that old God until his last hour."

The last of the popes, with only his recollections of God to sustain him, had climbed the mountains to have a last festival, as became an old pope and church father: "a festival of pious recollections and divine services." And he had found that other old saint, too. "Now, however, is he himself dead, the most pious of men, the saint in the forest, who praised his God constantly with singing and mumbling."

"Is it true what they say," Zarathustra asked the pale old man who had served God until the last, "that sympathy choked him?" The old man did not answer. "Let him go," said Zarathustra. "Let him go, he is gone."[98]

Belief in God does not fall alone, a single star from the sky. It carries a cosmos with it. It *is* a cosmos of meaning, of commitment, of behavior. A world with a God, deprived of God, is chaos. It is as if the Ptolemaic belief that everything orbits about the earth had suddenly lost its power to convince, and nothing were put in its place. One would not know what to expect or how to act. Nietzsche said that a world deprived of God, a world accustomed to seeing *that way*, is a world without moral structure. God guaranteed the *truth*, made truth *divine*. "But what if this belief becomes more and more incredible, what if nothing proves itself to be divine, unless it be error, blindness, lies—what if God himself proved Himself to be our oldest lie?"[99] That would mean that a new problem exists, "the problem of the value of truth." Morality simply goes to pieces. Nietzsche suggested that would produce a great hundred-act play that would occupy Europe for the next two centuries. If he was right, we have seen scarcely half the drama.[100]

The English, Nietzsche thought, make it a habit to indulge in a modicum of theological liberation. In England, the realization of the loss of God results in a curious kind of terrifying moral fanaticism:

They are rid of the Christian God and therefore think it all the more incumbent upon them to hold tight to Christian morality: . . . That is how they do penance in that country. [English readers need not feel particularly put upon; Nietzsche had little good to say about anyone else, not even other Germans.] Christianity is a system, a complete outlook upon the world, conceived as a whole. If its leading concept, the belief in God, is wrenched from it, the whole is destroyed; nothing vital remains in our grasp.[101]

Christian morality rests on a command. The commandment goes with the commander. Nietzsche thought that when the situation was finally realized, universal madness would break out. "Is there still an above and below? Do we not stray, as through infinite nothingness? Does not empty space breathe upon us? Has it not become colder? Does not night come on continually, darker and darker? Shall we not have to light lanterns in the morning?"[102]

Nietzsche was not sorry to see Christian values go, whatever the chaos it caused. Historically, Christianity won a war of morals, and in that conflict a nobler type of character was destroyed, Nietzsche thought. In its place, he said the church aimed at producing a typical decadent. Nietzsche argued that his studies of the classical world demonstrated that two kinds of morality clash over and over again. He called them master-morality and slave-morality.[103] Moral distinctions, he said, originated either in a ruling caste, which was pleasantly aware of being superior to the ruled, or among the ruled class, composed of slaves and dependents of all sorts. It is the rulers who determine what "good" means. The noble man, the "good" man, distinguishes himself from those who are less exalted than he. He despises the timid, the insignificant, the distrustful, the self-abasing, the mendicant flatterers, the doglike kind of men who let themselves be abused, and liars. Nietzsche thought it was a fundamental belief of all nobility that common people, subservient people, were untruthful. " 'We truthful ones'— the nobility in ancient Greece called themselves." The nobler type of man is proud, regards *himself* as the determiner of values, does not require outside approval, and passes judgment. He, Nietzsche thought, is the creator of values. Almost by definition, then, the nobler man is "good" and the subservient, self-debasing man is "bad." Nietzsche believed that moral judgments about good and bad originated in the recognition of the differences between noble and subservient men. That is master-morality.

On the other hand, the slave has his own morality. The slave exalts all those qualities which serve to ease his own situation: sympathy, the helping hand, the warm heart, patience, diligence, humility, and the like, for those are precisely the qualities that make it easier for the slave to be a slave. They are not intended to *end* slavery, just to *ease* it.

Christianity, Nietzsche said, is a slave morality. It is, in fact, the most successful of all slave moralities. Nietzsche did think that at the heart it was really Jewish. For instance, to say " 'Only when thou *repentest* is God gracious to thee'—that would arouse the laughter or the wrath of a Greek: he would say, 'Slaves may have such sentiments.' "[104] God, in that relationship, is really a nobleman of such power and greatness that only his honor could be offended. Every sin is an infringement of proper respect. "Contrition, degradation, rolling-in-the-dust,—these are the first and last conditions on which his favor depends: the restoration, therefore, of his divine honour!"[105] Everything is interpreted as an offense to the divine majesty, not against one's fellow man, and if it pleases his majesty, he forgives the sinner, indifferent to the consequences against mankind: "all deeds are to be looked upon *solely with respect to their supernatural consequences*, and not with respect to their natural results."[106] Sins are regarded as against *God*, not man. God has merely been substituted for the noble man, and Christian morality perpetuates, even makes virtue of, the condition of slavery.

Preachers of morality try to persuade otherwise healthy men that they are ill unto death and that a severe, final, radical cure is necessary. After centuries of preaching that message, men begin to believe it, and the opinion that the human race is in a bad way is commonly held: "they find nothing more in life and make melancholy faces at each other, as if life were indeed very hard *to endure*."[107] Nietzsche thought there was good historical warrant for preachers talking that way:

Again I remind you of St. Paul's 'the *weak* things of the world, the *foolish* things of the world; and *base* things of the world, and things which are despised': this was the formula, *in hoc signo* decadence triumphed.[108] . . . Christianity is the revolt of all things that crawl on their bellies against everything that is lofty: the gospel of the "lowly" *lowers*.[109]

He thought the ideal saint would be a eunuch.

Nietzsche magnanimously revealed that toward the past he could be profoundly tolerant, could exercise "a sort of generous self-control," and not hold a thousand-year history of Christian mankind "responsible for its mental disorders." But *now*, he said, *now*: "Our age *knows*. . . . That which was formerly merely morbid, is now positively indecent. It is indecent nowadays to be a Christian." Theologians, priests, and popes *know*, and knowing makes them liars: "Even the priest knows quite as well as everybody else does that there is no longer any 'God,' and 'sinner' or any 'Saviour,' and the 'free will,' and 'a moral order of the universe' are *lies*."[110] To be able to go on as if nothing were different is to have lost the last shred of decency and self-respect, to have forgotten how to blush.

He said:

I *condemn* Christianity and confront it with the most terrible accusation that an accuser has ever had in his mouth. To my mind it is the greatest of all conceivable corruptions. . . . It converted every value into its opposite, every truth into a lie, and every honest impulse into an ignominy of the soul. . . . Its very existence depended on states of distress; it created states of distress in order to make itself immortal. . . . I call Christianity the one great curse, the one enormous and innermost perversion, the one great instinct of revenge, for which no means are too venomous, too underhand, too underground and too *petty*,—I call it the one immortal blemish of mankind.[111]

So Nietzsche believed that the real threat to genuine morality came from those who called themselves "good." The "good" crucify anyone who devises his own virtue; they sacrifice the present for some imagined future. *"Break up, break up, I pray you, the good and the just!"*[112]

"That which defines me, that which makes me stand apart from the whole of the rest of humanity, is the fact that I *unmasked* Christian morality."[113]

What then? The good and the just, Nietzsche said, called him the destroyer of morality. He thought himself to be anything but that, although he wore the title with pride: "My story is immoral."[114] Christian morality was not only content to remain slavish; it created slaves. Nietzsche proposed a new man, a noble man, a superior man.[115] He said a new nobility was needed. Man is something that needs to be surpassed. "Lo, I teach you Superman!" The Superior Man, in contrast to Christianity with its hopes for superearthly hopes, will be the *meaning* of the earth. Christians, he said, are the despisers of life, the decaying and poisoned ones. Once it was the greatest sin to blaspheme God, but God died, and now the greatest sin is to blaspheme this earth, this life. Man needs to learn to love himself with a wholesome and healthy love, to become what Nietzsche imagined noblemen of old were: proud, confident, truthful, the fashioners of morality. If God were dead, someone *must* fashion a new ethic. All the familiar ethical landmarks are loose, flying in the air: God is dead.

Nietzsche's analysis of the source of Christian and superior morality (slave and master) is both interesting and naïve. To be sure, there is a good deal of subservient mentality in Christian ethics. Every preacher knows how hard it is to get his congregation to transfer their feelings of offense against God to action in the world. Almost every church service is rededication to the inadequacy of man over against the Father in heaven who had higher hopes for him, but who, if one is sincere and subservient, will be gracious and forgiving. Paul Tillich, for instance, agrees that when one speaks of selfless love, and when one wants to sacrifice himself for the other one, this is only a way for the weaker person to creep under the protection of somebody else. It is a form of exploiting love, self-surrender in order to exploit.[116] And Nietzsche knew that with all the landmarks flying, something new had to be done. He imagined—quite naïvely, I think—that superior men, noble men, *masters* are themselves independent of the kinds of social pressures and approval for their own opinions and actions that apply to subservient men. But he was absolutely right that one cannot remove God as the sanction for ethical behavior without putting something in that place, and in that place Nietzsche wanted to put man himself; a *better* man, a *higher* man, a *Superior* Man, but *man*. That takes courage. There is not much to suggest that man is capable of bearing the load that God formerly carried. It may have to be done, but in the final analysis not even Nietzsche could bear it. That is part of the power, of course, of the God idea. It is by definition, more than man; infinitely more. Nietzsche knew it would be hard.

After Buddha was dead people showed his shadow for centuries afterwards in a cave,—an immense frightful shadow. God is dead: but as the human race is constituted, there will perhaps be caves for milleniums yet, in which people will show his shadow.—And we—we have still to overcome his shadow.[117]

Nietzsche tried to overcome the long shadow of God with his doctrine of eternal recurrence. That idea is clearly, for Nietzsche, a substitute for religion, "an attempt," Karl Lowith says, "to leave 'nothing' and arrive at 'something.'"[118] Nietzsche believed that everything will eventually be repeated again. That has happened and will happen again. Now that could be a gruesome thought, but the force of that belief is intended to cause us to be responsible. It is, as Lowith elsewhere points out, a way to be able to rejoice at our all too-human, too-fleeting, actions. It is a criticism of both the doctrine of creation and of the liberal chatter about progress.[119] There is a built-in contradiction in the idea, too. Unless one's present actions are free, able to affect the course of the movement of things, one might as well relapse into that morality of endurance Nietzsche called "slave." He clearly did not think one ought to be passive that way. If, on the other hand, one ought to will to power, to become more, to "surpass man," then the action must produce a new thing, a new state of affairs that has not been before; hence not eternal. The doctrine of eternal recurrence represents a loss of nerve, on Nietzsche's part, to do what he proposed to do: to be moral without God. The eternal recurrence acted quite like a God for Nietzsche. It gave him courage to be and to do what he had to do. It enabled him to face the fact that life was short almost beyond grasp. It will all come again.

That is not to dismiss Nietzsche. Oh, no! Far beyond his latter-day successors he saw clearly the consequences of living in a time of the death of God, of living without God. Everything unhinges. Everything is loose. There is a void, and darkness over the deep, and man stands alone, absolutely alone, on the edge of madness.

CHAPTER 3

One
Who Stole
Holy Things

I suggested earlier that the affirmation of the death of God is one of the contemporary God problems. Whatever it means, and it obviously means a lot of things, it is part of the way we come in our quest for God. If the sense of the absence of God is one part, the other part is the suspicion that God-talk is a peculiar way of talking about *something,* and something important. If, in this family tree we are sketching, Friedrich Nietzsche is one of our patriarchs, on the other side of the family the lines go back to Ludwig Feuerbach. As with Nietzsche, Feuerbach did not argue about the absence of God. Instead, he proposed that talk about God was really an unusual kind of talk about man. As was the case with the other men we reviewed, I will not attempt to summarize everything Feuerbach had to say but will focus on his explanations of what talk about God is all about.

If Nietzsche found it easy to secure an academic position, Feuerbach found it almost impossible. He was dismissed from his first position as a docent (lecturer) for anonymously publishing a book that spoke unkindly about Christianity. But if Nietzsche had few admirers, Feuerbach had many. One might also make comparisons of literary style that would be unkind to Feuerbach, but that would be a mean thing to say about a man who, when once challenged to a duel, replied that he would rather go to Heidelberg and give a lecture on religion.[1] A man like that cannot be all bad.

He was born in Bavaria in 1804 and, after first studying theology, studied philosophy under Hegel. His relationship to Hegel is important because in a sense he stood Hegel's philosophy on its head—or on its feet. Feuerbach reacted against those elements of Hegel's philosophy that gave priority to mind over the material world. That was, of course, to meet Hegel straight on. Hegel believed mind to be the *really* real, which Feuerbach found to be a denial of the real nature of man. According to Hegel, human reason is the way absolute being realizes itself, which, Feuerbach again thought, made ordinary human existence something less than substantial. Everything was invested in rationality, and in the final analysis all rationality was the work of absolute mind realizing itself. In response to that, Feuerbach asserted that Hegel had gotten the subject and the predicate reversed. *Being* is the subject, Feuerbach said, and thought is the product. Being is not produced by mind. Nature produces mind; mind does not produce nature. Beginning with the ordinary, sensual, material world, in effect committing himself to that as the basic, unquestionable reality, Feuerbach believed that *all* mind is a product of material reality, even what religious people call God's mind. The "personality of God," for instance, is nothing else than the projection of human personality. The *process* of projection was a Hegelian doctrine, except that Hegel would have said that man's consciousness is the consciousness of God realizing itself.[2] *Man* thinks, Feuerbach said. Man is the measure of reason. His implacable reversal of the dominant Hegelian scheme is seen in this impassioned plea:

Do not wish to be a philosopher in contrast to being a Man; be nothing more than a thinking man; do not think as a thinker, that is, with a faculty torn out of the totality of the real being of man and set up as something in and for itself! Think as a real, living being, as one exposed to the vivifying and refreshing surge of the sea of worldly experience; think in existence, in the world as a part of it, not in the vacuum of abstraction, like an isolated monad, an absolute monarch, an indifferent god! Then for a certainty thy thoughts will be unities of being and thought.[3]

"Man, that is, man's essence, is the most real being . . . , not the Ego of Kant and Fichte, not the absolute identity of Schilling, not the absolute mind of Hegel. . . . I hate," he said, "the Idealism which tears man out of nature."[4]

"To be a *man*," to affirm man, to free him, to help him know himself, to "see": that was the ambition and the intention that drove Feuerbach. He wanted, he said, to change "the friends of God into friends of man, believers into thinkers, worshippers into workers, candidates for the other world into students of this world, Christians, who on their own confession are half-animal and half-angel, into men—whole men."[5] In spite of the surface hostility of that statement, Feuerbach was a theologian by commitment and interest who did not see himself as an enemy of Christianity. He believed, on the contrary, that he had found the secret to genuine and productive religious life: "Certainly my work is negative, but, be it observed, only in relation to the unhuman, not to the human elements in religion."[6] Feuerbach never imagined himself an obstruction to genuine faith, although his opinions lost him the only substantial academic post he held, and by the time of his death he was regarded as either too supernaturalistic for the socialists or too humanistic and too atheistic for the theologians. In reporting the issuance of a first volume of a new edition of his works, a German news magazine said that one hundred years after his death (in 1872), many modern theologians see in Feuerbach their forerunner. Once considered the "church father of all free thinkers," he has become one of the church fathers of this century.[7] Feuerbach would have understood that. "Thus do things change," he said. "What yesterday was still religion is no longer such to-day; and what to-day is atheism, tomorrow will be religion."[8]

Now it is tomorrow.

"Brutes have no religion." Nineteenth-century men liked to call other animals brutes. We have since discovered that brutish behavior is better a description of the noblest animal of them all: man. (Our nobility is a sometime thing. So, fortunately, is our brutality, or there *would* be no way around Auschwitz.) On the strength of Cuvier's analysis of comparative intelligences, Feuerbach denied, as older writers had maintained, that the elephant was religious. (If Cuvier should by the slimmest of chances prove to be wrong, every graduate program of history of religions in the universe will be devastated. Comedians will recite the faculty minutes verbatim.) Although he does not use the term, Feuerbach argues that the essential difference between man and other animals is the ability of man to transcend himself, to see himself as an object of his own thought. Feuerbach uses the term "consciousness," although he admits that, in a simpler way, animals are conscious, too. "Consciousness in the strictest sense is present only in a being to whom his species, his essential nature, is an object of thought. The brute is indeed conscious of himself as an individual . . . but not as a species. . . ."[9] Man can talk to himself. Man alone, Feuerbach thinks, is capable of exercizing thought and speech—which almost by definition suppose another individual of the species—completely alone. "Man is at once I and thou; he can put himself in the place of another, for this reason, that to him his species, his essential nature, and not merely his individuality, is an object of thought."[10]

Feuerbach argued, with the dated kinds of psychology and science available to him, that the ability to transcend oneself, mentally to stand outside oneself and see what it is to belong to a species, is a kind of experience of infinitude. To know one belongs to a species is to know that individual life has a beginning and an end. It is to be conscious in a way that is larger than one's own life. Feuerbach calls that a consciousness of the infinite. A lesser animal, without that kind of self-consciousness, has not even the faintest awareness of an infinite being, Feuerbach maintained, because his level of intelligence (or his lack of ability to transcend himself) will not permit it. Human intelligence, which makes self-transcendence possible, is able mentally to imagine a kind of infinite perspective on human life. It is important to remember that that infinite perspective is a function of a completely finite, completely natural, completely human mind.

The mind objectifies things. That is a peculiar way of saying that thinking organisms are able to recognize *other* things. Man, by virtue of the complexity of his mind, is able to think about himself thinking—that is, is able to make himself a kind of object for his own thinking. The seduction in that process is to think that man as his own object is two things: a finite man, a member of the species; and something infinite, able to know beyond both beginnings and ends. Our mind does that, but when it does so we choose between them and yearn to be the infinite one. That, too, is a function of the mind, judging that a human mind *able* to transcend itself is better than something *not* able to transcend itself. "Consciousness is self-verification, self-affirmation, self-love, joy in one's own perfection."[11]

Whether what seems to us to be an experience of infinite vision *is* infinite is quite another matter. "The leaf on which the caterpillar lives is for it a world, an infinite space."[12] In a curious kind of way the caterpillar is in and by itself infinite. The limits of the world of any being are apprehendable only by another being above him. Man's experience of self-transcendence is a particularly bewitching one, then, because in a sense we are caterpillars who have learned to see that our world is leaf-large, and, knowing that, the temptation is to regard our own ability to *see* that as a kind of superior being. It is bewitching because it is *we* who see, and who are seen. Our apprehensions of infinity, then, are really apprehensions of the functioning of our own minds. "The absolute to man is his own nature."[13]

Human beings are clearly not infinite. We are conceived, born, and live three-score years and ten; if strong, four-score. In our saner moments that is one of the things we know best. But *knowing* that may be part of the problem. The complexity of our own minds—minds able to think about themselves thinking—has given us the measure of our own boundaries. In a fascinating, abstract way, that is to be larger than we are. To use a term Feuerbach uses, the ability to transcend ourselves is almost something separate: he regards it as a "screen" on which we project things. What we project onto this screen are our own experiences of "infinity." "Man first of all sees his nature as if *out of* himself, before he finds it in himself. His own nature is in the first instance contemplated by him as that of another being."[14] Because we know *we* aren't infinite, we are bewitched into regarding our own ability to transcend as if it were another *being*, an infinite being who sees us. "God" is the name for an infinite being. "God" sees us. "Religion, at least the Christian, is the relation of man to himself, or more correctly to his own nature (i.e., his subjective nature); but a relation to it, viewed as a nature apart from his own. The divine being is nothing else than the human being. . . ."[15]

"God" said Augustine, "is nearer, more related to us, and therefore more easily known by us, than sensible, corporeal things."[16] Feuerbach might almost agree to that because, as he explained it, "the personality of God is . . . the means by which man converts the qualities of his own nature into qualities of another being,—of a being external to himself. The personality of God is nothing else than the projected personality of man."[17] Hegel had it the other way around: God's personality was realizing itself in the mind of man. Hegel's most basic assumption was that the "really real" was absolute mind and that other reality was derived from that. Feuerbach assumed that natural man, unadorned by causes and prior explanations, was the basic reality and that "God" was a function of the way men thought: we invest our own ability to stand apart from ourselves as objects—"others"—with divinity. We call it "God" because of the way we purify and idealize our transcendent selves into something perfect over against our obvious imperfections as real, live human beings. And we give reality to "God" because "whatever a man conceives to be true, he immediately conceives to be real."[18]

"The yearning of man after something above himself is nothing else than the longing after the perfect type of his nature, the yearning to be free from himself, *i.e.*, from the limits and defects of his individuality."[19] God has a great deal to do with ethics, as Feuerbach understands it. This ability to stand apart from ourselves, and to see ourselves as if we were some other thing, is also what makes it possible for us to make value judgments about ourselves. To be able to reflect on ourselves in that way, to be able to imagine alternatives and to see consequences, is to be aware that we might be otherwise than we actually are. And to know we might be otherwise is only half a step from articulating what that "otherwise" might

be. What might a better man be? He would be a man with
our good qualities distilled and our bad qualities removed.
That, said Feuerbach, is precisely the way we describe God.
To objectify our moral judgments in God is, in a strange and
abstract kind of way, to declare those moral judgments to
have priority over us.

Every man . . . must place before himself a God, *i.e.*, an aim, a
purpose. The aim is the conscious, voluntary, essential impulse of
life, the glance of genius, the focus of self-knowledge. . . . He who
has an aim has a law over him; he does not merely guide himself;
he is guided. He who has no aim, has no home, no sanctuary; aimlessness is the greatest unhappiness. He who has an aim . . . has
. . . a religion.[20]

In religion Feuerbach wrote, man frees himself from the
limits of his life. He discards what oppresses him, or obstructs
his better intentions: "God is the self-consciousness of man
freed from all discordant elements; man feels himself free,
happy, blessed in his religion, because he only here lives the
life of genius, and keeps holiday."[21] In affirming that personality is an essential attribute of God (who wants an impersonal
mechanistic God?), man is, in effect, affirming that his own
personhood is an absolutely good thing. "In the personality of
God man consecrates the supernaturalness of his own personality."[22] To say, for instance, that God is love is, as Feuerbach understood it, an affirmation of the absolute goodness of
love. God as love is the wish of the heart, a wish exalted and
affirmed as a certainty before which no contradictory claim
can maintain itself: *God* is love. There are no claims so large.
"God is man's highest feeling of self, freed from all contraries
or disagreeables."[23] The things we attribute to God are the
best things of man, purified, blown large, and given a status
higher than our own, but they are *our* attributes, our aims, our
ideals. "Religion is human nature reflected, mirrored in itself."[24] Those things that we value, which we call perfect, those
excellent qualities which delight and claim us, those we say
belong to God. "God is the mirror of man."[25]
So, then, we are the animals blessed with rationality, with
self-transcendence. We can gain a perspective even on our-

selves. We think not only about ourselves thinking but about the whole species, and what we value and affirm about it. Goodness, love, truth, personality, beauty, graciousness, and whatever else we affirm we raise to divine status. In the same manner, we deny those meaner characteristics that seem to us to be destructive of human existence, deny that they are divine, and in that way make judgments that stand over against us. To use the broadest kind of language, we deny that God is evil: God is not irrational, he is not impersonal, he does not ignore the widow and the orphan. God is not just man blown large. He is the best of man, absolutely affirmed, without limitation and without spot or blemish. "What a man declares concerning God," Feuerbach said, "he in truth declares concerning himself."[26]

But that is just half the way in which religion moves. Onto the "screen" of our own "experiences of infinity" (our self-transcendence) we project the best of human aims, experiences, and ideals. Then (and this is the second half), having created the ideal, we act as if that ideal projection were itself the *subject* of our "relationship" and behave as if we were the *objects* of divine attention. "Man—this is the mystery of religion—projects his being into objectivity, and then again makes himself an object to this projected image of himself thus converted into a subject."[27] Feuerbach compared it to the working of the human heart: "In the religious systole man propels his own nature from himself, he throws himself outward; in the religious diastole he receives the rejected nature into his heart again."[28] First man creates God in his own image, and then, given an infinite kind of validity and existence by our own commitments to those things that constitute the essence of "God," God creates us in his image. Having been given custody of all our absolutes, God stands over us, for *we* have no absolutes: all the absolutes we attribute to God are the creations of the human mind. We aren't absolutely good, but *God* is: we have made him so. He, then, is greater than we. We don't live forever, but *God* does: we have made him so. We aren't absolutely just, but *God* is: we have made him so. In every way God is greater than we, and we are finally held in the palm of his hand, content to know that his graciousness is everything we wish for ourselves. First we objectify God, then personify God. The result is a supreme being over against whom we are less in every way.

Theism—the notion of God as a person or a personal being —is not a subsequent trivializing of the idea of God, not if Feuerbach is correct in his analysis of the dynamic of religion. It is common for theologians to protest in the name of all that is holy that the unsophisticated notion of God as a kind of person like us, only finer in every way, is a crude apprehension of what God *really* is. But according to Feuerbach, at the heart of the religious experience, God is precisely man blown large: "it is supposed that we have here unfolded to us the life of a Being distinct from us, while nevertheless it is only our own nature which is unfolded, though at the same time again shut up from us by the fact that this nature is represented as inherent in another being."[29] At the very base of religious experience God is manlike. Religious language about God is ambiguous, though, because at the same time that religion is an affirmation about man, it is also an abstraction from particular men, and this abstraction tends to depersonalize the concept of God, too. The process of abstraction makes us uneasy thinking of God as person, but still, at the heart, human personhood is the model on which God is conceived. For that reason, "crude concepts" of God as a person who does what people do persist with real and legitimate power. And for the same reason, when theologians try to qualify what personality or personhood means for God, it becomes very difficult to explain what they are doing or what is left when they have finished. The discomfort at unabashed theism is a legitimate expression of having come to know better what God-talk is all about, but the attempt to refine that language into something more abstract and less personal cannot finally succeed, because it ignores the fact that God-talk is built on a human model. As long as God is conceived to be "out there" or "down there" or "in here" somewhere, then person-language is the most natural way to describe God. "Simple Christians" ought not to be scolded for using appropriate language for that kind of God. If God is *not* another being, then, of course, one might do well to give up both plain and abstract being-language to speak of God.

Feuerbach said that God-language and heaven-language

are very closely related, almost two ways of talking about the same thing. Heaven is an expression in terms of place of what God expresses in terms of person. Feuerbach uses belief in immortal life as an example. To believe in life eternal is to say that God is eternal. God is the guarantor of immortal life, or better, the manner by which that belief is expressed. The same claim can be made by expressing belief in heaven. That, too, is an expression of faith in eternal life. God is the pledge of heaven, the anticipation of heaven. God, Feuerbach says, is the idea of the species, which will first be realized in the other world: heaven. "God is heaven spiritualised, while heaven is God materialised, or reduced to the forms of the senses."[30] To believe that man is immortal, Feuerbach says, is to believe that man is, or can be, divine, and belief in God is belief in personality released from all earthly limits, consequently divine. "As surely as there is a God," Feuerbach argued, "so surely is there an immortality. God is the certainty of my future felicity. The interest I have in knowing that *God is,* is one with the interest I have in knowing that *I am,* that I am immortal. God is my hidden, my assured existence."[31] God is the power by which man realizes his future existence, a future existence in which he will be one with God.

Further, as man imagines heaven to be, just so does he imagine God to be. The content of heaven, described as a kind of place, is expressed as God, described as a kind of person. Feuerbach believed that Christianity, in a variety of ways, was opposed to marriage. He regarded the adoration of the virgin, the New Testament advice against marriage, the celibate clergy, and monastic orders, as evidence for the opposition of the church to marriage. It is an unholy thing and is therefore excluded from heaven. "That which man excludes from heaven he excludes from his true nature. Heaven is his treasure-casket."[32] The fact that people marry on earth is not a refutation of that. On earth the Christian has to make many accommodations. "But watch for him when he throws off his incognito, and shows himself in his true dignity, his heavenly state. In heaven he speaks as he thinks; there thou hearest his true opinion. Where his heaven is, there is his heart,—heaven is his heart laid open."[33] Heaven is the true and the good; but earth is the untrue and the unlawful. Feuerbach believed Christian talk about heaven to be the key to the deepest mysteries of Christian faith. "As God is nothing else than the nature of man purified from that which appears, whether in feeling or thought, a limitation, an evil; so the future life is nothing else than the present life freed from that which appears a limitation or an evil."[34] The conception of a God is both an articulation of an ideal state of being and a rejection of actual human behavior. Man negates himself as he is in order to affirm himself either by speaking of God or of heaven. Both God and heaven are expressions of the goal toward which men strive. God and heaven (or heaven) is the wish of the heart made objective. "The Christian heaven is Christian truth. That which is excluded from heaven is excluded from true Christianity. In heaven the Christian is free from that which he wishes to be free from here—free from the sexual impulse, free from matter, free from Nature in general."[35]

Sounds awful.

To say that men are related to God, then, is just a curious way to speak about the relation of men to that which they judge to be good. "That which has essential value for man, which he esteems the perfect, the excellent, in which he has true delight,—that alone is God to him."[36] Religion comes with both blessings and curses. It is a blessing to be in a good relationship to that which we value, to the perfect and excellent, to that in which one finds true delight. And, on the contrary, it is the highest crime to doubt those things, to deny them. It is, in the plainest sense, to deny the best of our own humanity. It is a crime against our own good. If our own good is God, then to deny God is the greatest of all crimes. Only a fool would do that.

Feuerbach believed that he had shown that to speak of God was to distill those qualities that men believed to be their highest and best, those things toward which they aimed and to which they committed themselves, and to imagine those things as if they were external to man. We are judged by those qualities, those aims, those commitments we make. We measure our humanity by them. And because, by definition, they are better than we, and because we affirm those things to take priority over our actual behavior, we speak of those things *as if* we were children before them. We invest those ideals, those goods, with personality, and call it "God." "God" is our father.

The father is what the child is not. He is for the child what the child cannot be for itself. The child is dependent, unfree, incapable of caring for and protecting itself; but what it is not in itself, it is through its father—free and independent. The child does not have to beg, does not depend on the will of strangers, and is not nakedly placed against the attacks of hostile powers; it is cared for and sheltered. With the help of its father it goes through all dangers just as confidently as the man who depends only upon his own power and judgment. The power of the father is the child's power. The child cannot attain for itself what it wishes; but by means of its father it is master and lord of the things it wants. The child does not feel dependent upon its father. I feel dependent only upon a despotic being, not upon one who loves me; I feel dependent only when I am unwillingly dependent, in opposition to my impulse toward freedom. But the child is joyfully a child; it has in its father its self-esteem (children are proud of their parents), and it has the feeling that its father is not a being for itself, but rather a being for it, the child. The father has only physical power; but the true power, the one which determines and rules the physical ability to act, the child has in its hands—namely, the father's heart. As a man, as a being perfect in power and understanding, the father stands over the child, but only to stand under the child as father—that is, in his heart. The father is only lord of the child in order to be able to be the servant of its needs and wishes. The heart is the ruler of the earthly, as of the heavenly, father. But where, then, does the real distinction between father and child lie? Only in this: in the father there is present as an object what in the child is only a propensity; in the father there is actuality, whereas in the child there is only a goal for future development; in the father there is something present which in the child is something future; in the father there is something actual which in the child is a wish and a striving. The child determines itself according to the father; the father is its model and its ideal. In short, the child has in its father what it will possess as a mature man; except that it has in the father *outside* itself what it will later have *in* itself, and that what later will be in the child as its own nature is now presented in its father as a being separated from the child. The father is and says what that child is to be, can be, and will be. The father is the natural prophet of the child; he is the promise (already fulfilled in him) of the future lying before the child and already hovering before the hope and imagination of the child.

God is that object which holds up before man his own nature, which only calls out to man what he himself (*i.e.*, man) is. . . . God is thus nothing but the essence of the human heart—or, rather, emotion—objectified to itself as the supreme, truest, and most actual being.[37]

But calling God a supreme being does not make him a supreme being, and Feuerbach believed he had uncovered the secret of the Christian faith. "We have reduced the supermundane, supernatural, and superhuman nature of God to the elements of human nature as its fundamental elements. Our process of analysis has brought us again to the position with which we set out. The beginning, middle and end of religion is MAN."[38] God exists only in the heart of man, and it is delusion, Feuerbach said, to look for a real, external objective immortality, a God outside ourselves. More than that, it is an evil. On the contrary, he found it liberation to overcome self-delusion and to live honestly and truthfully for those things we can and choose to commit ourselves to.

The secret of theology is anthropology. . . . The necessary turning-point of history is therefore the open confession, that the consciousness of God is nothing else than the consciousness of the species; that man can and should raise himself only above the limits of his individuality, and not above the laws, the positive essential conditions of his species; that there is no other essence which man can think, dream of, imagine, feel, believe in, wish for, love and adore as the *absolute*, than the essence of human nature itself.[39]

That "essence of human nature" is, of course, as Feuerbach said, not just what man is but what he *aims* for.

Feuerbach said that to do what he did, to find the key to the Christian religion, to untangle true Christianity from the

web of contradictions and delusions called theology, was to
have committed a sacrilege. And if it were thought negative,
irreligious, and atheistic, "let it be remembered that atheism—
at least in the sense of this work—is the secret of religion
itself. . . ."[40] The *real* atheist, he said, is the one to whom love
and wisdom and justice—all those qualities men attribute to
God—are nothing. They are given to God because men have
found those things to be worthy of the idea of God. To deny
them is to be the unbeliever.[41]

"What yesterday was still religion is no longer such to-day;
and what to-day is atheism, tomorrow will be religion."[42]

He who says no more of me than that I am an atheist, says and
knows *nothing* of me. . . . I deny God. But that means for me that
I deny the negation of man. In place of the illusory, fantastic,
heavenly position of man which in actual life necessarily leads to
the degradation of man, I substitute the tangible, actual, and consequently also the political and social position of mankind. The
question concerning the existence or non-existence of God is for
me nothing but the question concerning the existence or non-
existence of man.[43]

It is the case that Feuerbach was at his weakest when he
looked at actual man. Karl Barth could not really make up
his mind whether, having read Feuerbach, one had heard
something extraordinary or merely something trivial.[44] (Karl
Barth was never modest in criticism.) He agreed that Feuerbach was a true child of the nineteenth century, who did not
know death and who did not properly know the evil man is
capable of. In Barth's theology, the death and evil of man
led Barth to conclude that there was no possibility of salvation in man, that *only* God could rescue man. He wondered
whether Feuerbach's "man" were real man.[45] Barth believed
that the essential difference lay in choosing whether or not
one believed man could do what Feuerbach thought man was
capable of, or whether God had to come in grace to save.
But that does not establish God. That is only to admit that
if man is that hopeless (remember Auschwitz?), nothing is
to be done for him. A healthy perception of evil and death
does not establish the existence of God as another reality.

Karl Marx also criticized Feuerbach precisely at the point of his conception of man. He said that when Feuerbach had done his work, the chief thing still remained to be done. To discover that the earthly family is the secret of the holy family is not enough. What remains is to *change* the earthly family to eliminate the evils that affect it. "The philosophers have *interpreted* the world in various ways; the point however is to *change* it."[46] Marx did not think Feuerbach even realized that. Perhaps.

But Ludwig Feuerbach is not refuted by arguing that his understanding of man is inadequate, or too optimistic, or that he does not go far enough in attempting to change the human situation. It might even be true that the situation of man without a supernatural God is completely hopeless. That does not touch Feuerbach's central contention. One would only have to conclude that the situation of man was completely hopeless, and we might just as well all go and shoot ourselves. If talk about God really is a peculiar but important way to talk about man, if God is not another being, or even the ground of being, then no amount of either pessimism *or* optimism will alter the fact that, as Jacques Monod says, we are alone.

And we are alone. Ludwig Feuerbach may or may not have written the best anatomy of religious language. Perhaps Christianity is as anti-natural-world as he says it is. Perhaps not. Perhaps he is too optimistic about man. Perhaps Richard Rubenstein is too pessimistic. They both have their reasons. And it may be the case, too, as I suspect, that Feuerbach confined his analysis of man too much to the interior of man, however much he protested (in passages I did not examine) that man and nature belonged together. Feuerbach may have known it first, but we do live in the time of (or after) the death of God. Nietzsche, even more than his successors, knew that the death of God (the awareness that we are alone) signaled the need for a radical rethinking of man's place and values. Feuerbach, even before Nietzsche, reminds us still that when people talk about God they are talking about *something*. That is important. God-talk may not be discourse about a being, or about being-itself, or about the ground of being. "Being-itself" or "the ground of being" is just as abstract a notion as "God in his ineffable wisdom," and no amount of similarity of language should allow us to equate any of those terms with man, of flesh and blood, life and death, love and grief. God-talk may simply be what Feuerbach said it is: talk about man, important talk about man.

It is clear: when people seriously have said "God" (whatever they meant), they usually intended to say the most important things they could express. Talk like that deserves attention. After all, even though Ludwig Feuerbach stole holy things, he did say "God," and he meant something when he said it.

CHAPTER 4

With
the Drawbridge
Up

The old saint who went out into the forest to seek roots, who praised God with singing, weeping, laughing, and mumbling, simply did not know that God was dead. Zarathustra hurried away lest the old saint should learn. The last pope knew, and he grieved. But when, on a bright morning, one came into the market place, carrying a lantern and telling of the death of God, the people laughed, all in a hubbub. They called him a madman. "I come too early," he said. "I am not yet at the right time."

Some of the people are still laughing. Some are still singing and weeping and laughing and mumbling, and thus praise God. Even William Hamilton, who says he *knows,* thinks he feels like celebration and comedy. That's good. Sometimes people laugh at funerals. Death makes people do curious things. Death is a terrible threat, and to try to imagine a world without God is more threatening still.

I would like to suggest that quite a lot of what is going on in theology today, and in religious practice, too, is a curious but entirely understandable reaction to the kinds of things madmen have been telling us.

In the preface to one of his books, Carl Braaten wrote:

In the long run it may become evident that radical theology has been having a cathartic effect on the church and its theology. The "death of God" phase may have helped to force theology to find a new beginning. I am a partisan in this quest for a new way to start theology. Therefore, while I am unable to count myself, and few others would wish to number me, among the radical theologians, I feel myself closer to them than this book, or any of my other writings, can adequately indicate. Their questions are always in my mind.[1]

Braaten is not a radical theologian in the sense in which that term applies to men like Altizer or Rubenstein. As a matter of fact, he is a profoundly conservative man, who argues eloquently and tenaciously that theology has to find a new starting place because, if that is not done, the church will not be able to conserve the treasures that it has or live out the mission that is proper for the people of God, a mission it has come desperately close to losing; "we can hardly go on the way we have been going."[2]

Carl Braaten is the most articulate and aggressive American proponent of what is commonly called the theology of hope or of future, sometimes the theology of promise or of revolution. In Europe, Jürgen Moltmann, Wolfhart Pannenberg, and Johannes Metz are the best-known articulators of this general movement in theology. They are not agreed in what they say. (Theologians generally, but European theologians particularly, consider it a matter of honor *not* to agree with each other. There is a clumsy passage in Moltmann's *Theology of Hope* in which he labors valiantly to show how what he says is really very different from what Pannenberg says. German theologians do not learn from each other. I am not sure, but I think they commune only with God and historical research.) Because he wrote a book with that name, Moltmann is easily associated with the theology of hope. The term hope does not precisely describe Pannenberg's theology; "future" or even "history" better describes the kinds of things he talks about. And Metz probably prefers the term political theology to suggest the interest he has in articulating a theology with a focus on our life in society. The distinctions are genuine, but they are not important for what I am doing here.

I want to examine the way that general theological movement talks about God. They do talk about God in powerful ways. I intend to let Carl Braaten be a spokesman for what I will (to his chagrin) generally call the theology of hope, or of hope and future. Braaten is more inclined to represent Pannenberg than Moltmann, and he does that with verve and clarity (precisely what Pannenberg needs, too). I will, though, let those two European genitors of the theology of hope speak for themselves as it seems wise. Someone else can establish their territoriality. It is their understanding of what "God" means that interests me.

Not everyone agrees that "we can hardly go on the way we have been going." Not everyone agrees that theology needs a new starting place. One could probably make a pretty good case that most Christians are inclined rather to keep things the way they have long been; to speak of God as Moses and Aaron, or at least Paul, did. Moltmann says, "Nowhere are men so conservative and so attached to the old as, of all places, in the church. There seems to be an unconscious desire in religion, at a time when everything is changing and is being renewed, to find one last bastion of continuity, tradition, and immutability."[3] But of all the attempts within the church to come to terms with the new situation that our time in history presents to us, the theologies of hope and future are easily the most impressive. That is not to say they are enough. They aren't. But they are creative, and they are strong, and they need to be dealt with precisely to see if they are adequate for the large demands of contemporary thought.

"The new place to start in theology," Braaten says, "is at the end—eschatology."[4] One of the striking facts of biblical scholarship in the last generation or so has been the clear realization that first-century Christians and their writings are saturated with expectations about the end of the world (or some such thing) that most contemporary men do not share. Nineteenth-century Protestant theologians did theology as if the intention of their work was to get a clear picture of who Jesus was and then somehow to emulate his life-style. It was Albert Schweitzer who pointed out that Jesus and his contemporaries looked at things very differently than we do. Jesus expected the world to end in some way, *soon,* and the kingdom of God to be established. Not only Jesus but the New Testament documents, too, were forged within those kinds of expectations. Twentieth-century preachers who insist that the New Testament plainly speaks of an early end to the ordinary business of the world are absolutely right. It is very difficult to ascertain what Jesus himself thought, because Jesus didn't write the New Testament. Other men, who in retrospect came to startling conclusions about him, tell us what they had come to believe. It takes very sophisticated biblical scholarship to separate the subsequent value judgments of New Testament authors from Jesus' own self-estimation. The results are meager, but insofar as one can be fairly confident, it seems to be the case that Jesus regarded his own ministry as a prophetic announcement and preparation for the early establishment of the kingdom of God. It is easier to establish the fact that the early church plainly expected history to culminate soon. Paul's advice about the inadvisability of getting married in light of the imminent coming of Jesus again is the most commonly recognized example of the church's expectations. He didn't come back, of course, and the fact that Christians *did* marry, and even took care to record their beliefs and experiences for subsequent generations, are the result of realistically coming to terms with that disappointment. It is foolishness *now,* centuries later, simply to reiterate what those earliest Christians discovered was not true. Even if Jesus *were* to return on the clouds next Tuesday afternoon and surprise us all (none more than me!), that still would not be what the earliest church expected. A nineteen-hundred-year error is, in this case, no mere detail.

Although it was Albert Schweitzer who almost single-handedly destroyed nineteenth-century optimism about imitating Jesus (or distilling Jesus to get an ethic we could apply to our own life transactions), although he was more than clear that Jesus and his disciples were concerned with the imminent radical transformation of the world, Schweitzer himself, for all practical purposes, ignored his own findings. His philosophy of reverence for life simply does not grow out of those apocalyptic affirmations. Moltmann argues that part of the reason for ignoring the eschatological framework of New Testament life is because eschatology was interpreted as having only to do with a last day or last things but was essentially unrelated to normal, ongoing historical life. It became the special province of fanatical sects and revolutionary groups.[5] When eschatology *was* studied, it was interpreted in "vertical" ways, as the breaking in of eternity from above into time here below, an interpretation that robbed it of its orientation as a future event in time. If it is true that time has invaded our consciousness as much as these theologians of hope believe, then theology itself must also be constructed in terms of time and history, not in vertical ways. Eschatology is really about hope, Moltmann argues, and hope is forward-looking and forward-moving. The expectation that something dramatic will happen soon has the effect of turning the believer forward into the future, expectantly. Whether what is expected is anticipated sooner or later, it still remains that the proper response to that expectation is the reorganization of one's life toward the coming time. Paul expected Christians to meet Jesus and go to heaven with him and to live there without sexual relationships. So he advised his readers not to marry *now*. His expectations for the future had historical consequences. That Paul was utterly wrong about the eschaton is not the point here. An eschatological outlook is, at bottom, an attitude toward the remaining time and how it ought to be used in light of an anticipated state of affairs. Jesus spent himself trying to get people to reorganize their lives in anticipation of the kingdom that was coming, probably soon. The interpretation of eschatology as an attitude toward history, as a way to live in time, and not primarily as an astounding last event about which we can only be amazed, has enabled the theologians of hope and future to appropriate what earlier seemed a colossal mistake. Moltmann says, "There is therefore only one real problem in Christian theology, which its own object forces upon it and which it in turn forces on mankind and on human thought: the problem of the future."[6]

Ernst Käsemann says that apocalypticism is the mother of all Christian theology.[7] That is obviously not true, or he would not have to persuade those other Christians whose theology denies it that he is correct. But it is a way to affirm the legitimacy of using those New Testament materials that are clearly anticipatory of a new kingdom of God in the world. The theologians of hope agree that Jesus and Paul and a lot of other Christians obviously were wrong about their timetables. That can be denied only by the most awkward and abusive mental contortions. They do, though, affirm that the kingdom *is* at hand, is coming, and they do that in very peculiar ways (more about that later).

It is undoubtedly no accident that, at the same time they affirm that an attitude of hope toward the future is of the essence of the Christian faith, they also suggest that contemporary life is concerned precisely with questions about the future. And there you are! A correlation of biblical and contemporary concerns that would have made even Paul Tillich proud! "What is needed today," Braaten writes, "is a new correlation between the eschatological origins of Christian faith and the present revolutionary forces that seek to build a new and better future for mankind."[8] The Christian gospel, Braaten writes, can expect to get a hearing in contemporary culture only if it has some important news to bring about the human future, when it is concerned about the world's tomorrows. A faith that has nothing to say about the future will be disregarded.[9] To the extent that the Christian lives eschatologically—that is to say, to the extent he lives hoping for a radically new tomorrow—he shares a great deal with the culture around him, which is also a future-oriented society. Moltmann says that "since 1789 the land of 'utopia' no longer lies somewhere beyond the seas, but by means of the belief in history and the idea of progress it is shifted to the future which is possible and is to be expected or desired. The utopian dream has thus become a part of the philosophy of history."[10] Not only utopians but also the whole revolutionary surge toward liberation is fed by the dream of a better tomorrow. "The future-less and hope-less outlook of a generation ago is no longer the dominant mood in our culture."[11] The whole new situation that black people in America created for themselves is the result of a change in attitude toward their own possibilities. A little hope is a dangerous and powerful thing. It fuels revolutions. It certainly has done that for black America.

Hope is what people do when things look bad and no

guarantees for something better are evident. Hope, then, almost by definition, is the anticipation of a better state of affairs. Hope, except in the rarest of circumstances, is not an affirmation of the status quo. That, in itself, is a shock to a church that has heavily invested itself in keeping everything safe and in order. The message of hope, Braaten says, is that man is in distress. If the church takes seriously its hopes for the qualitatively new, it will find itself standing with an uncomfortable array of the world's outsiders who demand a change for the better. It may be at that point that the theology of hope will be most seriously tested. It will not matter whether the church is being true to its eschatological sources or not, if in trying to be the radically new it discovers that it must turn on itself. One could argue fairly persuasively that the church has shown precious little interest in revolutionary change. The church in the Soviet Union is a good example of a church that chose to ally itself not with the revolution but with the status quo. Part of the godlessness of the revolution must be attributed to the refusal of the church in Czarist Russia to champion the peasant case against what seemed to the poor to be an oppressive government. "Hope," Braaten says, "is on the lookout for something really new, and will not model the future on the past and the present."[12]

Hope is not a pipe dream, though. "Hope alone is to be called 'realistic,'" Moltmann says, "because it alone takes seriously the possibilities with which all reality is fraught."[13] There ought to be a tough-mindedness about hope that knows that history is more than what it appears to be at any moment. To hope is to believe that history is pregnant with unanticipated children.

One could argue persuasively that the character of the world around us is an anxiety for something better than what we have. "What if they gave a war and nobody came?" That is the genesis of a new world. What if we used our money to feed every hungry person instead of food-stamping them to death? What would happen if we really *wanted* to make cities places for human beings to live? What would we do if we took human justice seriously? That is the tender head of hope looking around, and hope like that grows up to become a radical revolution. The theologians of hope think that the church by nature ought to be able to speak to these issues, because to be Christian is to anticipate a new heaven and a new earth. There is some disagreement about whether the kingdom is really *this* earth renewed or not. An otherworldly hope is not exactly what the nonreligious world has in mind. Whether or not the future that theologians are committed to is the same future that the restless non-Christian hopes for is at least as important as any purely formal anticipatory stance they both assume. If they are not pointed in the same direction, the energy of their commitments to change will only produce a terrible collision. If that happens, it would have been better had they both rested on their status quos. It is simply not as clear as Moltmann and Pannenberg and Braaten and company would like to think, that their understanding of the future and the future to which revolutionary forces in the world are committed sufficiently correspond. That will be particularly evident when we examine just what the theologians of hope expect the future to bring.

Braaten argues that the whole death-of-God phenomenon is the result of the abandonment of eschatology. "If we speak of God apart from the future, then we are paving the way to speak of the future apart from God."[14] And then, citing Eugen Rosenstock-Huessy, "When people consider God as having been our maker in the past only, and abandon eschatology and a belief in God's future, their belief in God's presence disappears too. So Nietzsche, finding a Christianity devoid of faith in Last Things, rightly shouted, 'God is dead!' "[15] That is a curious argument because it supposes that God used to do things, now doesn't, and consequently he doesn't matter. That makes sense. But only by the most unusual perspective is that a loss of eschatological perspective. It is a complete loss of *God,* and loss of God (who once acted) is simply a loss of God, now, tomorrow, or whenever. That, to use Rosenstock-Huessy's term, is not just "a Christianity devoid of faith in Last Things," it is a Christianity devoid of God at all, and that is what Nietzsche said. Braaten argues, "To say that God is dead may be only a different way of describing a theism in which eschatology had died."[16] Those theologians who are saying that God is dead—and the theologians of hope are clearly not among them—aren't simply rejecting a God grown senile and inactive. As we have seen, they believe a variety of things about God. Altizer believes in God, and one who is acting and will act. It is hard to know what Hamilton really believes, and Rubenstein just cannot make himself believe that the God in whom Abraham and Isaac and Jacob trusted is there at all. There is no evidence. There is, rather, Auschwitz. Did Nietzsche lament the loss of faith in Last Things? A good clear exposition of Last Things would have *confirmed* Nietzsche in his opinion that people must find some other basis on which to live and create values. Theism died (for those for whom it *did* die), not because of a lack of interest on the part of the Almighty in the future, or because people *imagined* God was not future-oriented, but (to use one of Braaten's images) because it was "an inevitable casualty of Occam's razor in a scientific age."[17] That is to say, there was a simpler explanation: not that the conception of God was inadequate in certain respects, but that supposing there were no God at all made the most sense. (Graffito: "Occam had a beard.")

Braaten is absolutely right that God, if there is God, if the hypothesis makes sense, had better have something to do with our future, and our future interpreted historically, not in the medieval categories of natural and supernatural places. Whether or not that is possible remains to be seen. But he is correct: "For modern man transcendence will be understandable in terms of his orientation to the future or not at all."[18] But even that may be just an indirect way of saying that if there is a God he will matter. It remains to be seen whether God, as the theologians of hope and future speak of him, will survive Occam's razor. The formal coincidence of mutual interest in the future will not, in itself, be persuasive. As Moltmann himself acknowledged, "The recognition of the eschatological character of early Christianity made it clear that the automatically accepted idea of a harmonious synthesis between Christianity and culture was a lie."[19] Much more important, I think, than the coincidental interest in the future is the question of whether their talk about God is persuasive, whether their descriptions of the world and our lives make sense to people who do not come with any particular interest in defending the idea of God for historic or nostalgic reasons. The theologians of hope do speak of God in interesting ways. As is most clear in the theology of Pannenberg and Braaten, they have shifted basic categories, from talking about God in terms of being to talk in terms of future, or perhaps in terms of the future of being. That shift was made possible, in large part, by use of the philosophy of Ernst Bloch.

"Without Ernst Bloch there would probably be no hope school."[20] Bloch is not a Christian. He is a Marxist, with reservation. Chiefly through his work *Das Prinzip Hoffnung,* he has changed the way most of the hope theologians look at the world. None of the hope theologians share his atheism (that will be clearer later), but all of them think differently because of him. He has stimulated a powerful theological movement, not because of the clarity of what he says but because of the perspective from which he sees everything. He is a visionary, and vision eludes logic. He believes that man first dreams his future, then anticipates and moves toward it. Man is a kind of pilgrim who hopes ahead of himself, and who, because he hopes for something that is not yet, is (figuratively, at least) pulled along by the future. What for Bloch is a figure of speech, or a stance toward the future, becomes something more concrete for the theologians who use him.

Man is not just an individual for Bloch. "Just an individual" almost doesn't exist for him. Man is part of a commonwealth of humanity, a commonwealth that does not yet exist in finished form. The commonwealth is both a goal of man and an actuality that presently exists largely in anticipation and hope. In that sense, individual persons now act in response to something that does not yet exist. The source is ahead of us, not behind us. The "promised land" is not an original garden or a place apart from the historical process. It is a future possibility. To speak peculiarly, the "commonwealth of freedom" lies ahead in history, "pulling" voyagers toward a goal that can only be dreamed or hoped for. Time, then, is a kind of process that is going somewhere in particular and which, although it *could* be aborted, Bloch thinks will not be. In that sense he sounds a great deal like Teilhard de Chardin. The process moves forward, collecting all the earlier contributions toward the dream, always becoming more than it was. The end point is a new thing.

The individual is not so real as the commonwealth, for Bloch. That is not to say that the individual is nothing, but for him man is first of all a member of a human community, and as a member of the community he continues to exist even after he dies. It is hard to know precisely what Bloch does mean. He seems to believe in something like reincarnation without all the connotations of personal identity. Life somehow extends beyond death, and "we live over and over. ... Not at all times, but intermittently—and above all at its end—we live the entire life, the broad, historical life that is assigned to 'mankind' as a whole."[21] There is a lot of Hegel still floating around in Bloch. The point is that Bloch understands human life as a whole, and our real identity is to be found as part of the commonwealth toward which we commit ourselves and which, as it is realized, defines who we really are.

The world, then, is a process. It moves. History is a journey. Everything is defined in terms of time. We move toward something future, not toward some other, perhaps supernatural place. Capps says:

Thus, man understands himself to have been placed on a continuum, a continuum marked by the integers of time. Because of the continuum, the future emerges as something entirely credible, and as something to which man has access. The continuum's capacity to remain flexible—at least flexible enough to admit a future which, in a chronological sense, is "still not yet"—gives realism to man's hope.[22]

Bloch speaks of the goal of mankind—the commonwealth of freedom—in two kinds of ways, and because he does that he is enabled to play little word games with the ideas of history and man's participation in it. On the one hand he speaks chronologically: the commonwealth still lies ahead of us in history. That is pretty ordinary talk. It still is not yet a reality in that sense; it is anticipated. On the other hand, he speaks psychologically, or in terms of human intention. The goal in that sense is present. We commit ourselves to it and, in doing that, participate in it. When Pannenberg and Braaten apply that kind of language to the kingdom of God, they tend to blur the distinction in those ways of talking and speak of the kingdom as if it somehow sat out there in the future and pulled us along. It "causes" the present. That will be clearer in a moment.

Bloch's dream of a commonwealth is not guaranteed; it has to be realized. For that reason, human activity is important. New things must happen before it can exist in historical actuality, and the new things will be effected by people who share the utopian vision of their predecessors and contemporaries, and whose actions together with them move history along toward that goal. Bloch is a Marxist, but his quarrel with Marx is precisely at this point. Marx believed that economic circumstances determined the situation and future of man. That, Bloch argues, does not allow for evident human effectiveness: "Man does not live by bread alone. Outward things, no matter how extensive their importance and our need to attend to them, are merely suggestive, not creative. People, not things and not the mighty course of events outside ourselves . . . write history."[23] The gods are gone for Bloch, and it is for people to fill the vacuum left by divine intentionality.

Philosophy, as Bloch does it, is concerned for what can be or, perhaps stronger, what will be. The commonwealth lies ahead, not above. It is the work of man, not God. It must be moved toward, brought into being by as yet unrealized hopes and dreams. It is at this point that the theologians part company with him. Bloch agrees with Feuerbach that "Man is the God of Christianity, and anthropology is the secret of Christian theology."[24] God is not in the sky, he is really the goal of the world, as men hope for it. Braaten is clear: he thinks matter cannot bear the weight of God; it will collapse.[25] "Bloch is a humanist; his denial of God as an independent existing being is motivated by his interest in the radical humanizing of religion."[26] That is an important comment because it clearly expresses something about God as the futurist theologians speak of him. God, for them, still is "an independent existing being." The castigations of old-fashioned theism are frequent in their writings, but the fact is they still are theists. What they reject is the notion that God is sitting on his majesty somewhere, doing nothing. What they say instead is that God—independent, existing, being—is out there in the future, doing his thing, and doing it here too. Let us turn to that.

It may be helpful to examine what it is these theologians reject concerning belief in God. At first reading they seem to want to reject theism. Braaten writes (for himself as well), "Traditional theism has not been able to withstand the onslaughts of radical questioning, Pannenberg believes, precisely because in its formulation the notion of the futurity of God and his kingdom was prevented by the Greek idea of the eternity of God as a timeless presence without change."[27] But as we said a moment ago, his open disagreement with Ernst Bloch was precisely at the point where he charged Bloch with denying the existence of God as an independent being. When we turn to his positive definitions of God, we shall see that Braaten particularly likes to speak of God as the Power of the Future or in closely allied terms. The similarity to Tillich's terminology is deceptive (Power or Ground of Being). Tillich specifically rejected theism. God was not a being for Tillich. He is for these men, or if he is not a being he is something so similar that the distinction eludes me. God laughs. In a brief assessment of the death-of-God theologians, Braaten points out that most of the establishment reactions to quash the revolt of those radicals have been justified. He cites their glaring weaknesses: lapses into logical positivism, misappropriation of a "blik," no good reason for preferring Jesus, an arbitrary canon, and visionary language. And more, it is humorous. "One redeeming feature of the new discussion about God, no doubt, is the humor that runs throughout. If one happens to believe in God at all, he cannot help but hear echoes of the laughter of God intermingling with his own most serious thought about God."[28] Perhaps that is just a figure of speech, although it is difficult to imagine the Power of the Future chuckling. We may never know. We do know, according to Braaten, that God does suffer. In a discussion of the relation of Jesus to God, Braaten is careful to emphasize that Jesus is not a replacement for God. The suffering of Jesus on the cross does not preclude the suffering of God at the same time: "We do not believe in an impassible God—a God who is stone cold in his heart of hearts toward the suffering of his creatures. Only a suffering God can help."[29] Braaten says he finds the idea of a God in pain important, and the ancient dispute about God not suffering to have bizarre consequences—a Father who does not respond to his son's anguish. "To believe in a God who does not suffer great pain," he continues, ". . . must mean that ours is a Greek deity for whom motion itself is most painful."[30] It is fairly clear that when Braaten rejects "traditional theism" he is really rejecting a static world view. Braaten does not like the traditional language about the perfections of God who is so complete that nothing can be added to his experience. He rejects the platonic distinction between this world of becoming and the perfect world of essences and thus, in the Christian appropriation of those categories, a world of change contrasted with a cut-glass God. And Braaten is right about that. Many of the tortured disputes of Christian theology have the causes for their being rooted in that impossible relationship between those supposed levels of reality. But Braaten is a theist. God is a being for him, a laughing, suffering, compassionate being who, to be sure, is not overhead in heaven. But like Dietrich Bonhoeffer, who denied that God existed out there or up there somewhere and who in consequence tried to bring God here into the middle of ordinary life, Braaten has only proposed to change God's location. He is Futurity; he is the Power of the Future. The question is whether a theistic God in time is much of an improvement over a theistic God in space.

Ernst Bloch believes that history is moving—as men move it and are moved by it—toward a commonwealth of freedom. The commonwealth is not yet visible. It exists only in anticipatory ways. Nevertheless, every free action of men toward that goal, as time will demonstrate, will be seen to be a part of the fullness of the commonwealth. The commitment to a future shapes present activity. What exactly will be the case, though, cannot be known until that dream is realized. Then, in retrospect, all preliminary activity will be recognized for what it really was. Where Bloch dreams of a commonwealth, the theologians of hope dream of God and his kingdom.

Braaten says natural theology has collapsed. For centuries

it had been assumed that an examination of nature could produce evidence of God. Arguments about God as first cause or
highest being or universal essence simply do not persuade.
Braaten calls those "counterfeit answers." "We can no longer
proceed in the old way from a God we already know, whether
that be the God 'up there' or 'back there' or 'deep inside,'
whether the highest being, universal essence, or first cause.
These gods of natural theology have lured believing Christians
into a posture of atheism."[31] What natural theology can do, he
says, is ask the right questions. Proofs for God are really questions about God. A "new style of natural theology" would not
attempt to establish God, his nature and his being, but would
articulate the questions that man has about his own identity
and meaning, about the future of both mankind and the
world. Those, Braaten thinks, are really questions about God.
"It is not natural for man to be an atheist!"[32] The question
"Who is God?" arises, he says, out of man's concern for his
future.[33] That is an interesting theory. It makes anyone who
asks questions about his future, anyone who wonders who he
is, a religious man, whether or not he wants to be one. "It
is not natural for man to be an atheist!" Is it not patently the
case that "God" is just one answer to those kinds of questions?
Is it not true that some people who plainly disavow both overt
and unsuspected Gods *have* answers to those questions? Paul
Tillich said that anyone who had an ultimate concern had a
God, and a lot of concerned atheists and agnostics got nervous.
Because they have defined God as futurity, or the power of
the future, the theologians of hope and future are able to
baptize absolutely anyone who wonders who he is and whether
things are going anywhere. "A person moved by the question
of hope for the future may discover that the biblical faith in
God speaks that same language."[34] The question is whether
they speak the same answer.

Reconstituted natural theology can only ask the questions
about the future. God can be known only through Jesus of
Nazareth: "Jesus' God will be his God, or he will have no
God."[35] That is going to come as a shock to a lot of non-
Christian believers in God. God is to be found through Jesus
because Jesus identified himself completely with the future
kingdom of God. Braaten prefers the term power of the future

to the terms kingdom of God or heaven, because those latter terms are too easily identified with traditional theism. The power once awaited from heaven we await from the future. "God's transcendence can be conceived today as the absolute power of the future. He comes to us not 'from above' but 'from ahead.' "[36] God, then, is the absolute power of the future. "Futurity is essential to his very being."[37] The term power of the future makes it possible to speak of God in relation to New Testament eschatological expectations about the coming kingdom of God.

"The power of the future" is an abstract-sounding term, but Braaten, at least (and the others, apparently), does not intend it to be just talk about a tendency, or open opportunity, or some such impersonal thing. He says that in his very being God is the common future of the world, the unifying force of all contingent events in nature and history. Contingent events, he says, may be thought of as chance happenings or erratic occurrences, "or they may be thought of as personal acts that spring meaningfully from the power of the future."[38] God is a self-identical unity connecting what seem to be chance happenings in a meaningful way. The future is a personal power. Pannenberg says that God is not an existing entity but is the future of his coming kingdom (the future of a future state!). That sounds like a denial of God as person, but in the context of their concerted denials of Greek ontology, it probably ought to be understood as the denial of a "Greek" supernatural God. Pannenberg is harder to pin down about that. He denies, for instance, that God as futurity implies any development in God himself; God is the ultimate future. That is terribly close to those old Greeks he wants to avoid, even if in one instance he is ultimate future and in the other ultimate being. Pannenberg agrees that the idea of the personal character of God is essential, but very difficult to discuss in terms of what people associate with the term.

When God is defined as the ultimate future, and what might otherwise be called chance occurrences are considered to be personal intentional acts, then one is close to affirming a future that causes the past to become something. Pannenberg, particularly, speaks that way:

What warrant do we have for saying that those contingent events are in fact acts of God from whose future they spring? In every event the infinite future separates itself from the finite events which until then had been hidden in this future but are now released into existence. The future lets go of itself to bring into being our present. And every new present is again confronted by a dark and mysterious future out of which certain relevant events will be released. Thus does the future determine the present.[39]

The future, Pannenberg writes, makes imperative claims on the present. Jesus' message was the claim that the coming kingdom of God was near and claimed us. "It is more appropriate to reverse the connection between present and future, giving priority to the future. . . . In this way we see the present as an effect of the future, in contrast to the conventional assumption that past and present are one cause of the future."[40]

Pannenberg presents an impossible option: does the past cause the future, or does the future cause the past? He says, "The past, we are taught to believe, brings forth the future according to the reliable laws which control events."[41] Braaten does the same thing: "The future does not grow out of the past; the present cannot be projected into the future as its determinant content."[42] So also Moltmann: "Does the present determine the future in extrapolations, or does the future determine the present in anticipations?"[43] These men talk a great deal about freedom, but when they present the options for the way things happen they present two rigidly determined systems. Either the past determines the future or the future determines the past. Neither of them prefers to think that the future will be more of what is presently the case (What kind of a kingdom of God would *that* be?), so they opt for the latter. Things just appear to us to be free and chancy. Really, God is personally acting himself out, unfolding himself in the present. Well, nonsense! Those are not the only options. The activities of the past clearly and undeniably structure *part* of our present situation. We are black or white, the air is polluted, half of the topsoil in Georgia has washed into the Atlantic, two world wars have been fought: all those things present us with some givens. In turn our present actions will in the same way present the future with situations within which it must operate. It is true that one sometimes, perhaps often, acts with an eye to future consequences of the action. Sometimes we have very long and large goals in mind when we act, dreams for the future of mankind and the earth. One could say, I suppose, that the future causes those events, but that is just a peculiar and misleading way of saying that we now, having certain hopes and dreams, act now to effect a future state of affairs, insofar as we can. One must always be modest about the ways one can shape the future. Other people, present and future, are just as shortsighted, wrong-headed, perverse, and free as we are. Within the relative givenness of their situations they may ignore our intentions, deny or contradict them, or perhaps even share our dreams. The relationship between past and future is much more complex than these hope theologians seem to suggest. What they may be searching for is a way to confirm what they hope: that the kingdom of God (the power of the future, or the absolute future) must necessarily come. Hope is not insurance, even from up ahead: it is just hope, but that is quite a lot. If one denies that contingencies are really contingent, then there has to be absolute causality, either from the past or, less plausibly, from the future. As Carl Braaten himself admits, thinking of the future as prior to the past and the present is likely to cause "hernia of the mind."[44]

He understands the problem.

Natural theology, properly understood, might help us to ask the right questions, but real knowledge of God is to be found only in Jesus. "If Jesus of Nazareth is the *self*-revelation of God, then this is the eschatological event after which there need not be another such revelation of God. Jesus . . . is our future as the eschatological event."[45] Since the divinity of Jesus cannot be asserted in the context of traditional Greek metaphysics, a new way has to be found. Pannenberg works it out most carefully. He agrees that the formulas of Chalcedon no longer convince. To say that Jesus is both a divine being and a human being in the same person is confusing because it suggests that humanity and divinity are equivalents: two beings complete in themselves cannot together form a single whole.[46] Pannenberg believes that the unity of God in Jesus can be understood only retroactively (just as he thinks everything is only to be understood). Jesus was a man—a real man—who lived completely in and for the future, that is to say completely in and for God. But that was not completely clear, even to Jesus, until the resurrection. The resurrection validated the complete union. "Until his resurrection, Jesus' unity with God was hidden, not only to other men but above all . . . for Jesus himself also. It was hidden because the ultimate decision about it had not been given."[47] For that reason Jesus did not claim more for himself than perhaps the role of an eschatological prophet. Apparently, as Pannenberg divines it, God always knew about that "ultimate decision" even though he had not yet given it. It was "always present to his eternity."[48] The attempt here is to avoid speaking of humanity and divinity as if they were on the same plane, but, same plane or not, "As this man Jesus is God, . . . he is one with God and thus is himself God."[49] As the man who was completely obedient to the Father, he revealed God's divinity and does himself belong to the essence of God. However, from the perspective of this life, that fact was apparent only from its end.[50] By his complete identity with God or with the power of the future, Jesus is, then, our future, the future of the world. To use a term all three men use, Jesus' resurrection is proleptic, a present instance of what will finally be true. There is still more to know about the resurrection, though. While Pannenberg insists that the resurrection had to be a historical event,[51] he admits that he does not know what "really" happened. "The ultimate divine confirmation about Jesus will take place only in the occurrence of his return. Only then will the revelation of God in Jesus become manifest in its ultimate, irresistible glory."[52] Jesus was wrong about the arrival of the kingdom in his generation. That occurred only proleptically in his own resurrection. And that is what we all await, Pannenberg says, when he comes again. That is the ultimate destiny of man.[53] He believes that the coming kingdom is not otherworldly: it is the destiny of present society.[54] Even though he stoutly insists the resurrection was *historical,* he concedes that only the eschaton will disclose what really happened.

Moltmann tries hard, too, to make the resurrection something historical, but he does it by redefining what is historical. All historical understanding these days, he says, is analogical.

We think we can understand the past because it is *like* something we know. That is to say, we have a particular world view. We assume events are similar. In that regard, the resurrection presents a special problem: "the risen Lord does not fit in with our concept of the historical."[55] It is not *like anything* else. There are no analogies. In order to make room, then, for an event like the resurrection, which simply does not fall within the boundaries of acceptable or *knowable* happenings, Moltmann says we need to reorder our sense of what we will accept as rational.

Then the theology of the resurrection would no longer be fitted in with an existing concept of history, but an attempt would have to be made, in comparison with and contradistinction to the existing views of history, to arrive at a new understanding of history. . . . The resurrection of Christ is without parallel in the history known to us. But it can for that very reason be regarded as a "history making event" in the light of which all other history is illumined, called in question and transformed.[56]

The resurrection, in this view, is "history making," not because it is something significant in history but because it remakes what will count as historical. As the theologians of hope understand it, the resurrection is an event without analogy in all of history, an instance of what the future holds for all of us: a new kind of existence in which death will be overcome. Resurrection is a new creation, Moltmann says, in which God will not create out of nothingness but out of this first creation. God himself will dwell in the midst of the new creation (Jesus is both human *and* divine), and there will be neither affliction nor pain nor work. We will play with God.[57] (Sounds like oodles of fun!)

None of these men knows what the resurrection *is*. It is the new creation, the new being, the ultimate future. Braaten says, "In affirming the event of the resurrection, we are not offering a theory to explain it. What is basic to the Christian hope is that it happened and what it means, not how it happened."[58] It is foolish, he says, to suggest that an explanation is needed to participate in what it promises. He himself tends toward a "transformation theory" in which Jesus was transformed to a new mode of reality. He is living with God in the future.[59] Agreeing that the resurrection faith is historically unverifiable, Jürgen Moltmann says, "But within history we do not live by such valuations, but by hopes and fears."[60]

I am afraid that is it.

I heard a radio announcer once describe what he was about to play as "a Mozart concerto in the style of Puccini. Of course," he said, "Puccini had not yet been born."

Of course. The theology of hope is a lot like that.

Somehow the theology of future has gotten everything backward. It isn't a theology of the future at all. It is a theology straight out of a distant past, scarcely retouched.

I have scarcely mentioned the finest part of the theology of hope, because I wanted to focus on what it says God is and means. The theology of hope, when applied to the society of which we are a part, is exciting. With its deliberate rejection of the status quo, and its focus of attention on the new things that must take place, it is a powerful instrument to move the church toward trying to be part of the solution to human problems.

But the apparatus that has been constructed to help the church up off its pew is incredible! These men have not found a way to correlate an eschatological New Testament faith with a contemporary future-oriented world. They *are* that first-century faith in, but not of, a contemporary world. Do they really believe in reverse causality? Do they really believe that God, out ahead in the future somehow, is teasing the world toward a predetermined future? Do they really believe that Jesus has been accepted by the Power of the Future and exists in the ultimate future? Do they really believe that Jesus will come again? Do they really believe that someday God will transform "the ontic condition of all things"?[61]

They do.

All these men have changed is the basic category by which they attempt to speak of God (from being to time), and they do not even do that consistently. They literally believe that God is a person of some kind, that he took Jesus up out of the grave and apparently ontically transformed him, that he will come again to transform the world, and so on. They find only one clear place where they take issue with what first-century Christians believed: Jesus was wrong about the kingdom coming very soon. But even there, he was half right, even if he didn't realize it. *He* became part of the new kingdom then, and he waits for us someday.

That is incredible. The theology of hope is first-century world view, once overcome by Greek ontology, purged of a good share of its static language, propelled forward into an otherworldly (or transformed-worldly) future. The theology of hope is a retreat from the twentieth century. It is subsequent to the death-of-God theology, but it is not "a new stage." It is a reaffirmation of a way of looking at the world and life that has become simply unbelievable for increasing numbers of people. It is just what it claims *not* to be: it is a *re*-newal, a *re*-affirmation, a *re*-treat. It is in the face of theology like this, fortified with enormous scholarship and men of clearly superior abilities, that people said God was dead. Are contemporary men required to reenlist in a world view that has lost its credibility? It cannot be done.

No one, seeing that the sun is in the center, can ever again live on a flat earth. Not even if Jesus did.

CHAPTER 5

In His
Image

After he had written *Honest to God,* John Robinson wrote another fine little book called *Exploration into God.*[1] Robinson agrees that theism—the concept of God as a person—is becoming increasingly difficult to affirm. That is not to suggest that no one is a theist or that intelligent people cannot be theists: it is, rather, to say that there is a growing uneasiness with theism. It is even very difficult to say who is growing uneasy. A generation ago, when Rudolf Bultmann proposed that modern men could not uncritically affirm biblical myths, he was reminded that many contemporary men did in fact do just that. He is reported to have replied that not all contemporary men are modern men. It is that way with theism, too. The issue will not be settled with a show of hands or by a Harris poll. An opinion poll is more likely to show, as Peter Berger reports for 1967, that 68 percent of the West Germans said they believed in God but 86 percent prayed to him.[2] When it serves their purposes, theologians play the poll game, too. "I don't know which modern men my opponent has in mind . . . ," it usually begins, and then friendlier modern men are cited. But in spite of all that, and in spite of Billy Graham, who talks to God, theism is a problem. I am not concerned, at the moment, to collect a list of reasons why theism perturbs. One might compose a very long list. For some of us it just won't work; we simply do not see the world that way. Nothing hangs together that way. It is a way of seeing everything that is as strange as trying to affirm a flat earth. John Robinson is one of those theologians (however many there are) who think that theism, once meaningful, is now a problem: "I am convinced that to represent the spiritual reality (in its transcendent aspect) as a Being in another realm is to make it unreal and remote for vast numbers of people today."[3] And again: "As a Being he has no future."[4] Robinson does believe in God, and he does try to avoid theism, and for that reason his argument is worth attention.

Robinson believes in God, but he does not believe God is a person. *In Honest to God,* Robinson had said that God was, by definition, ultimate reality and that one does not sensibly argue whether or not ultimate reality exists: "One can only ask what ultimate reality is like—whether, for instance, in the last analysis what lies at the heart of things and governs their working is to be described in personal or impersonal categories."[5] The ease with which Robinson speaks of the "ultimate reality" that "lies at the heart of things and governs their working" is evidence enough that his rejection of theism is not simultaneously a rejection of a theistic concept of God. Deeply influenced by Tillich's rejection of a theistic concept of God, Robinson argues that theism deserves to be discarded. It is, he agrees, an outmoded view of the world. "We shall eventually be no more able to convince men of the existence of a God 'out there' whom they must call in to order their lives than persuade them to take seriously the gods of Olympus."[6]

Robinson concludes that as *a Being* God has no future. He argues that the parallel with the Devil ("God's opposite number") is telling. The Devil, he says, has become a semicomic figure, regarded by most educated Christians as a mythological expression for the reality of evil. Life has a dark side to it for which the Devil is a mythological expression. "The irony is that by insisting on the ontological status of the Devil churchmen have powerfully contributed to the reality's being dismissed along with the supernatural figure."[7] In the same way,

Robinson argues, to insist on the ontological existence of God is merely to invite similar rejection.[8] But Robinson is not really willing to let God be the Devil's "opposite number." Were he to do that, he would have to call God the bright side of life, or the good side, or some such thing, and then the question would remain (as it really does) why God should not be explained in the same way that the Devil is explained. Why not, then, simply say that God (quite like the Devil) is a mythological expression which dare not be given ontological status lest it be laughed into dismissal? Robinson argues that our age is neither mythological nor ontological but functional. Evil (formerly expressed both mythologically and ontologically—a being) must now be expressed functionally (which Robinson, following C. A. van Peursen, thinks is characteristic of our time). But Robinson does not suggest that. His argument only works one way, and not on one of the "opposite numbers." The reason is that he thinks God, not convincingly expressed either mythologically or ontologically, *does* something, that is to say, is functioning; and the Devil isn't.

Like Tillich, who affirmed a "God above God,"[9] Robinson thought God could be found in deep down places. "When Tillich speaks of God in 'depth,' he is not speaking of another Being *at all*. He is speaking of 'the infinite and inexhaustible depth and ground of all being,' of our ultimate concern, of what we take seriously without reservation."[10] Robinson speaks a good deal about the "heart of things," which seems to be very much the same thing as those "deepest down things" made famous by Gerard Manley Hopkins and the "depths" of which Tillich wrote. Robinson also has an uneasy affair of the heart with mysticism. In spite of his protests that he really is not a mystic by temperament, he is nonetheless fascinated by the immediate experience of God mystics have always claimed for themselves. Robinson seems to use Martin Buber's concept of "I-Thou" to hold all these things together. At the middle of his religious life, providing the foundation for his theological reflection, Robinson is convinced of personal experience of God. His uneasiness with mysticism lies in the fact that he does not want to claim knowledge of God *as* God. Robinson has no blinding visions of God (at least none that he reports). But he does claim to have some sense of the presence of God somewhere down deep in life. He says it is an utterly intimate, personal relationship, best summed up by Jesus' use of Abba (Father or Daddy, Robinson says). "It is this relationship at the heart of the universe, at the very core of reality, for which Christian theology has to find expression."[11]

In a moving section in which he attempts to locate the reality of God, Robinson describes the experience which forces him to his theological position. Like Brigham Young arriving in Salt Lake City, there are moments, Robinson says, when the vividness of confrontation with bedrock reality is so overwhelming that one responds, "This is the place."[12] It is, he says, the consciousness of being encountered, of being seized, held by an objective reality. It comes from beyond oneself, speaking within oneself. The believer responds to this "objective" reality; the unbeliever does not: "The fact that life is conceived as a relationship of openness, response, obedience to this overmastering reality is what distinguishes the man who is constrained to use the word 'God' from the nonbelieving humanist."[13] It is very difficult to know in what sense the God experience Robinson describes is "objective." If he means that it is a verifiable event, he is either talking nonsense or denying his own admission that God is not a part of things that are—that is to say, just another being, however exalted and fearful he might be. Rather, I think, Robinson intends to assert the dimensions of his own conviction that he has felt quite as he describes things. "It is to acknowledge a relationship, a confrontation at the heart of one's very constitution as a human being, of which one is compelled to say, in existential terms, 'This is it.' "[14] God statements, then, are statements about the reality of that relationship.

To say of this or that situation, as the Biblical writers do, that "God" is in it is not to start making statements about some supposed metaphysical entity outside it or beyond it; nor is it to say simply "This piece of history is of fundamental importance for my life." It is to say that in and through this event or person there meets me a claim, a mystery, a grace, whose overriding, transcendent, unconditional character can only be expressed by responding, with the prophet, "Thus saith the Lord."[15]

There is a religious experience behind Robinson's theology. He is aware, as perhaps many people are, of a sense of being confronted by a "Thou." But he is canny enough in the midst of his experience to want to avoid two other kinds of experience. Deism is one of them, and pantheism is the other. Deism has its roots in the Enlightenment. As the scientific view of the world seemed to become more and more adequate for explaining what things are and how they operate, God was edged into the background of what seemed to be a marvelously self-contained world machine and finally relegated to the role of original engineer. "It produced," Robinson says, "a remote, artificer Deity standing in a less than truly personal relationship to his creatures."[16] On the other hand, Robinson is anxious to avoid pantheism. Whether or not it really makes any sense to speak of God identified with every thing that is, Robinson will have none of it. It fails to do justice to God's transcendence, he says, and it fails to account for human freedom and personal identity; pantheism tends to absorb everything into divinity.[17]

Robinson's rejection of pantheism is consistent, even though he tends to define it in such a way that the distinction between God and the whole universe seems to dissolve. Whether or not that is what pantheists have intended, Robinson rejects it. But what he sometimes calls the deistic alternative is not always called deism. Sometimes he calls it dualism. If pantheism is monistic, theism is dualistic. Reality, he believes, is "all of a piece."[18] There are not two kinds of reality, one natural and the other supernatural. Theism, even if it does preserve the transcendence of God, does so by creating two levels of reality, and that, Robinson believes, is decreasingly convincing. However much it tried both to protect the transcendence of God and to establish a connection between the two levels of being, "theism failed to establish a genuine reciprocal relationship between this Being and the world."[19] Concerned to safeguard the otherness of God, theism discredited what it tried to preserve. "God has been pictured as a super-Self, deciding to act, intervene, or send this, that, or the other, including his own 'Son.' "[20]

Robinson wants the best of both worlds. He wants to preserve the transcendence of God (God isn't just another name for something in the world), and he wants to avoid speaking as if God were an unnatural intervention in ordinary events (there is no evidence for that). So he concludes that God isn't separate from everything (theism), nor is he to be identified with everything (pantheism): he is *in* everything (panentheism). God is neither separated nor identified with everything. He is *in* everything, literally everything, and to be found only in things. God is both transcendent and immanent.

"The beyond" is to be found always and only "in the midst," as a function and dimension of it. This is a shot-silk universe, spirit and matter, inside and outside, divine and human, shimmering like aspects of one reality which cannot be separated or divided.[21]

And it is for that reason that Robinson can speak of being addressed, claimed, and sustained by an utterly personal Thou.

Robinson is interesting, because he knows a problem when he sees one, and he is honest. He is absolutely right about theism; it cannot be sustained, for increasing numbers of people. The notion of an omniscient, omnipotent, and benevolent God who governs this reality we call our world is inconsistent with what we actually find to be the case, particularly if he is supposed to be susceptible to the persuasion of human appeals for special attention, and if it is the case that human beings regularly offend and thwart him. Massive and nearly endless systems of thought must be erected to make that system work. And natural disasters, for which man's perversity can not be held responsible except by the most fantastic assertions (the thistles and thorns argument), are intolerable if there is a God who both cares and is competent to control them. If theism is intolerable on that account, pantheism is superfluous. If things are understandable without recourse to God, what does the assertion that God is, or is in, all things mean? Immanence without transcendence is meaningless.

Robinson, at least, asserts both transcendence and immanence, but that only creates its own problems. In spite of his charge that traditional theism was guilty of a kind of dualism that is becoming increasingly difficult to maintain—our reality and something beyond or above or beneath us—Robinson really does have two realities. God, he is quite clear in saying, is not just a way of talking about the world. There is a beyond in the midst of things, at the heart of things, and it is an utterly personal beyond, even if it is not a person. Robinson believes we are confronted by a Thou, and a Thou whose reality does not depend on the world being there. "The model of panentheism," he says, "is essentially an incarnational one."[22] Just what is that Thou? Simply naming it won't help. Is "God" just the name for mystery, awe, the sense of being confronted? I think not. If that were so, "God" would be just a name for some stirring but entirely natural things, and Robinson wants to deny that. But he also wants to deny that God is to be operative in the world. He wants the world to work by itself.

And what does it mean to say that God is not a person but is more personal than person? Robinson argues that God (incognito at the heart of things) is supremely personal but not a person. That is desperately near being nonsense. It is, at least, imagination run wild. What might it mean to be more tree than a tree? More light than light? Blacker than black? More personal than person? No. That will not work. Theists are right when they attribute superpersonhood only to a superperson. But Robinson properly recoils from the idea of a super-Self. Still he wants superpersonhood without the superperson. What is he talking about?

What about the experience of being confronted by an utterly personal Thou at the heart of things? Who has those kinds of experiences? Are they self-authenticating? When it happens does one just know that God has grasped one? Must it be interpreted? Can it be explained some other, less dramatic, less otherworldly way? What about the people who stoutly maintain that they never have had such an experience? Must one desire it? Must one qualify for it? Is it only for the few? If it has not happened, can one rest assured that it will happen in God's good time? If it never happens, is that a sign of divine disfavor?

I have the faint suspicion that the experience of an utterly personal Thou is something like the infinite qualitative distinction of neo-orthodoxy. One day all the neo-orthodox wondered all together what they were talking about: the Emperor had no clothes.

Robinson wants to talk about God. He is really talking

about a feeling. He *feels* confronted by God. He feels gripped, addressed, challenged, sustained. The feeling is real, but it is a feeling nonetheless. It is not qualitatively different from the report of a small child who cries out in the dark that he is afraid. He is afraid. Mothers usually gently argue that nothing is present in the dark that is not there in the light, but the child knows a real fear when he feels it. Sophisticated mothers might even be able to analyze the fear—something about being helpless in a large world, or about the need for love, or perhaps about death—but for the moment that knowledge will not replace simple assurance. Fear is a real feeling, even fear of bogeymen, even if bogeymen are not real.

Friedrich Schleiermacher tried to ground certainty about God on the feeling of absolute dependence. He knew that God is not action alongside other actions, that God is not available through special knowledge. Why do we talk about God? We have this feeling, he said, a feeling of absolute dependence. And it was true that a lot of people did indeed feel dependent on something or someone. Some still do. That is not appreciably different from feeling gripped by someone or something down there at the heart of things, in the middle of life. But *damn* Sigmund Freud! It was he who taught us how deceptive are our feelings. We feel things that are simply not objectively the case. It may be the case that there is an utterly personal Thou grasping at us from the midst of everything, or it may only be the case that we *feel* grasped; in the latter case one does not need to resort to constructing some other reality to account for the experience.

Robinson rests his case on his claim for an experience of God, but "there is no direct experience of God, only experiences which are interpreted in a religious manner."[23]

In his book *A Rumor of Angels*, Peter Berger proposed to come to terms precisely with the lack of direct evidence for God. A priest working in the slum section of a European city said he continued "so that the rumor of God may not disappear completely." That, Berger says, is what the signals of transcendence have become for us—rumors—and not very reputable rumors at that.[24] Robinson almost restricted himself to this natural, everyday world—at least was anxious to do so as much as possible. Finally, though, he was grasped by another presence. Berger is much more ready to assert a supernatural, but he is more reluctant to specify how or where one knows of it. Robinson, like quite a few people today, "felt" the presence of God. Perhaps it is that Berger knows how ambiguous are feelings. Instead of proposing to look for the supernatural directly, Berger thinks that the ordinary human world contains clues to something beyond this reality. "I would suggest that theological thought seek out what might be called *signals of transcendence* within the empirically given human situation. And I would further suggest that there are *prototypical human gestures* that may constitute such signals."[25] A signal of transcendence, according to Berger, is a natural phenomenon that appears to point beyond the natural to the supernatural, and prototypical human gestures are reiterated acts and experiences that appear to express something essential about man. What Berger, in effect, proposes to do is to talk about God without talking about God. It has to be done that way because there is no direct evidence for God. That is worth remembering.

Berger specifies five signals of transcendence, although that is not intended to be an exhaustive list: order, play, hope, damnation, and humor.

Berger thinks that a natural inclination toward order is of crucial importance for understanding man's religious situation. Every society, he says, is an order erected in the face of chaos; without order, faced with chaos, life is terror. "Throughout most of human history," Berger says, "men have believed that the created order of society, in one way or another, corresponds to an underlying order of the universe, a divine order that supports and justifies all human attempts at ordering."[26] To assert order in the face of the disorder evident in the world is fundamentally an act of faith, he says. When, for instance, a child wakes in the night and cries, alone and afraid, the mother is a high priestess of order. When she turns on the light, cradles the child, and sings, she is in effect saying, "Don't be afraid—everything is in order, everything is all right."[27] Of course, everything is not all right. Everything is not in order. "The world that the child is being told to trust is the same world in which he will eventually die. If there is no other world, then the ultimate truth about this one is that eventually it will kill the child as it will kill his mother."[28] But in spite of that the mother says it is all right, because, in the order of things, the *transcendent* order of things, Berger thinks, being can be trusted to overcome death. There is another world, and one can trust himself to it. The natural world is only the prelude to another world.

In the same way, one can argue from our tendency to play that something transcends us. Play sets up a small arena in which the rules which apply to serious affairs are suspended. In the serious world it may be eleven o'clock in the morning, but in the world of play it may be the third round, or the fourth act, or the *allegro*, or the second kiss. Play, Berger says, is an enclave within the serious world. To play is to step from one chronology into another, from time into eternity. "Joyful play appears to suspend, or bracket, the reality of our 'living towards death' (as Heidegger aptly described our 'serious' condition)."[29] As in his description of order, Berger describes play primarily over against death. Although the child, he says, does not consciously see play in relation to death, that is in fact the case; "the suspension is unconscious."[30] It is *at least* unconscious, one might say. Not to be aware of death at all is a peculiar suspension. When an adult watches children play hopscotch, it seems to the adult at least—perhaps to the children, too—that the outside world has ceased to exist. And for the adult onlooker, Berger says, that outside world, ruled by pain and death, might for a moment be suspended also as he is drawn into the spell of the game. Or again, when the Vienna Philharmonic played a scheduled concert even as Soviet troops neared the city, and when they resumed their schedule again with only about a week's interruption, that, Berger thinks, was "an affirmation of the ultimate triumph of all human gestures of creative beauty over the gestures of destruction, and even over the ugliness of war and death."[31] Play, in short, constitutes a signal of transcendence, because it points beyond itself and man's nature to a reality beyond.

The third signal of transcendence that Berger suggests, hope, is closely related to the first two. Man extends himself into the future, Berger says. That is to say, man realizes himself in projects. Hope finally points to something, not only beyond the immediate circumstances but beyond the general human condition.

Human hope has always asserted itself most intensely in the face of experiences that seemed to spell utter defeat, most intensely of all in the face of the final defeat of death. Thus the profoundest manifestations of hope are to be found in gestures of courage undertaken in defiance of death.[32]

The artist who in the face of death strives to finish his work, the person ready to risk his life for someone else, the one ready to sacrifice his own comfort for another hopes for human creation. "All these contain an ultimate refusal to capitulate before the inevitability of death."[33] It is evident that death is large for Peter Berger, and order, play, and hope (and, not quite so plainly, damnation and humor, too) are responses to our impending death. "There seems to be," Berger thinks, "a death-refusing hope at the very core of our *humanitas*."[34] (Why do people use foreign words where they serve no useful purpose whatsoever?) Driven toward death, men hope for another supernatural fulfillment of life.

It is a signal of transcendence that, in circumstances in which the fund of human outrage is insufficient for the offense, men curse in supernatural dimensions. "There are certain deeds that cry out to heaven."[35] There are *monstrously evil* deeds. It would have been inadequate, even inhuman, Berger argues, to view the Adolf Eichmann case with scientific detachment. To have restricted our actions to reasonable responses to the way Eichmann was reared, taught, and acted under the circumstances would have been a denial of the monstrosity of his actions as an executioner of Jews in World War II. Even the death penalty is inadequate: " 'Hanging is not enough.' . . . No human punishment is 'enough' in the case of deeds as monstrous as these. These are deeds that demand not only condemnation, but *damnation* in the full religious meaning of the word."[36] Just as certain gestures anticipate redemption, Berger says, so do other gestures anticipate hell, meaning damnation not only here but beyond the world as well.

Finally, there is the argument from humor. Following the suggestion of both Freud and Bergson, Berger suggests that humor is essentially the apprehension of a fundamental discrepancy, incongruity, incommensurability. Humor brings together two independent series of events in such a way that two entirely different meanings are possible. "Discrepancy is the stuff of which jokes are made. . . . *The comic reflects the imprisonment of the human spirit in the world.*"[37] When tragedy is laughed at, tragedy (for the moment, at least) is overcome. Humor implies that tragedy is not the last to be said; ultimately it will be overcome. Power, Berger says, mocks illusion, and power is the final illusion, while laughter reveals the final truth. The human spirit is uneasy in this world because it is at home elsewhere, and laughter is a recognition of that and a way of overcoming this reality. Religion vindicates such laughter.

Order, play, hope, damnation, humor: "There are some prototypical human gestures that appear timeless and that may be considered as constants in history."[38] Avoiding comment on "timeless" human gestures for the moment, it appears to be Berger's intention to avoid discussing the possibility of direct religious experience (whatever that could mean, presumably an immediate knowledge of God). Berger deliberately confines his attentions to whatever can be said about ordinary life that seems to hint that more is there than can be seen. There is absolutely no doubt that Berger thinks there is much more to the world than the world. The subtitle to his book is *Modern Society and the Rediscovery of the Supernatural*. There appears not to be the slimmest reasonable question in Berger's argument about that other reality which lies beyond this natural, evident, ordinary world. All of the signals of transcendence he explicates are suggestions to him that there is more. In that respect Berger affirms a world view that, for some of us at least, is much more than questionable. He believes that there is a beyond—some radically other reality—and he thinks that there are clues to its existence. His world view, then, is plainly the world view of long centuries of Western civilization, a world view partially shaped by Christian faith and shared by it. But it is not a contemporary world view. That is not name-calling. Neither is it to charge that no sensible man continues to see reality that way: Peter Berger does, and he is an eminently sensible man, and he shares his position with most Christians. But it is a dated world view as surely as the earth is not the middle of the universe. And Berger clearly knows he holds an increasingly unpopular position. He does not deceive himself about that, nor does he believe that fifty million Frenchmen cannot be wrong. He has consciously chosen to maintain a minority position (at least insofar at theologians these days can be considered a majority of anything).

Whether or not Berger believes that God can reveal himself directly, he probably accurately assumes that he will get nowhere with that argument, so he focuses on such clues as this self-contained, self-explanatory natural world seems to provide: his "signals of transcendence." In effect he claims that those five human habits (order, play, etc.), by their very nature, point us beyond this world. They do not demand acknowledgment of God—the world can explain its own—but they hint at something. Berger has a kind of Compatibility Theory: it is *compatible* with what we know of ourselves and the world to assume a supernatural realm. But what is not clear is why we should need to look beyond this world at all. Berger is not presumably proposing wild and interesting theories just for the fun of it. He must think that the assumption of a supernatural realm alongside this world makes everything "fit" better than the assumption that there is no such realm. That is to say, he thinks his world view better accounts for human experience than any alternate. One recalls Kuhn's discussion of paradigms. We really are confronted, in this whole discussion of God, and God as a being, with conflicting paradigms, with conflicting world views. And again, as Kuhn explained, one tends to argue out of the context of his own paradigm. Perhaps that is all we can do. It is clear that the signals of transcendence that Berger cites—surely those he finds most compelling—need not be interpreted as he does it at all.

Why not agree, for instance, that order, play, hope, damnation, and humor are quite as characteristically human and quite as important for understanding who we are as Berger says? But rather than proposing that they point *beyond*, why not simply say that they point to the way we are? We are the creatures who try to wrestle order out of chaos, perhaps as a function of our intelligence. We are the animals who play, but not the only ones who play. Sometimes we play to forget how tough things are, sometimes for the pure unadulterated fun of it! We do know outrage almost beyond bounds, the kind of outrage that makes us, when confronted with damnable behavior, do damnable things ourselves. We still think that killing each other is a reasonable way to stop people from killing each other. That isn't a signal of transcendence, a hint of God; that is outrageous! We are the beings who, because we have inherited exceedingly complex and entirely remarkable brains, know both that we were born and that we shall die, and we are the beings who find a macabre kind of chagrin in it all: we laugh. Play isn't an escape for little girls playing hopscotch: play *is* the world for little girls, just as it is for the Vienna Symphony or the New York Yankees. That *is* the world. That is *this* world. All the experiences of life, play and hope and damnation and all, are evidence for the joy and terror that constitute being here and being alive. Life is that way. It is enough to know that. It does not require another reality, or even another dimension of reality, to account for hope and humor and damnation. At least, that is the issue.

Berger is not alone. Langdon Gilkey argues quite as Berger does. In *Naming the Whirlwind,* he says:

The experience of the sacred and so our knowledge of what Christians name God are not separated from our secular life and values. The sacred is dimly but universally experienced by all men everywhere as a source of that life's power and joy, the source of its meaning and structure, and finally wherever that experience is known as the sole ground of that life's healing.[39]

Gilkey says that the life experiences that cause one to speak of God rather than just the natural world, or the universe, are of four general kinds. Each of them seems to him to suggest a quality of the unconditioned, of the infinite, of transcendence, of an ultimate. This quality of holiness or sacredness appears, first of all, as the *source*, ground, or origin of what we and everything finite are. It is the sense that our life is given to us and is finally not absolutely ours to control and to direct. Life is gift. In the second place, ultimacy (as Gilkey prefers to call it) shows itself in relation to our *limits*, when we feel an absolute threat and helplessness. When we experience the limits or the ground of life, in the sense that there is something there beyond our own finite existence, then we are touching on the borders of the ultimate. We experience that limit both positively and negatively, Gilkey says, both as the source of all we are and as an infinite Void that threatens to engulf us. Third, the ultimate is also the source of our *values*, he says. As a consequence, the loss of this sense or experience of ultimacy is also the destruction of all value; without value we are nothing. And fourth, there is an essential element of mystery in the experience of ultimacy, particularly because of the dialectic character of our experiences. The ultimate is both source and void, negation and affirmation.[40]

What is particularly evident in Gilkey's discussion of those life experiences that occasion God-talk is his insistence on their dual character. We experience not only ground, he says, but void. The presence of ultimate holiness is also the presence of ultimate condemnation.

This dimension or framework of ultimacy appears *directly* in the awareness of an unconditioned Void. . . . It is experienced *indirectly* in the joyful wonder, the creative meanings, and the resolute character of life despite its obvious contingency, relativity, and temporal character.[41]

In a long series of common human situations, Gilkey examines the occasions that produce our sense of being up against something that transcends us: the desire to be whole, to exult in life, love, birth, death, insecurity, cultural collapse, the search for meaning and purpose. In all of them Gilkey asserts the necessity of recognizing that there is more than the natural world there. There is a sense or experience of the other, of mystery.

Further, Gilkey believes the experience is a universal human experience. "The sacred is dimly but universally experienced by all men everywhere as a source of that life's power and joy, the source of meaning and structure, and finally wherever that experience is known, as the pole ground of that life's healing."[42] In a footnote to the passage just cited, Gilkey agrees with Frederick Herzog, not only that the experience of God (the sacred, the ultimate, etc.) is universal but that very often those who have the experience do not *know* what it is they are experiencing. Herzog: "Theological hermeneutic must stress that the immediate experience is not instantly known as God."[43] The experience of the sacred, Gilkey says, is both in and beyond the profane. It is to recognize an ultimate order behind and within ordinary experience, to know eternal good beyond and within the ambiguities of our life. It is "present, at least in dim awareness, wherever man is fully man."[44]

That is a nearly impregnable position, of course: everyone has an experience of God, but not everyone knows it. Men who are fully men know it, and not to know it is not to be fully man. Well, that is to bestow religion even upon the avowedly irreligious, and to call their inability to recognize it immaturity. Some integrity must be granted to that substantial band of honest people who know all the human experiences, all the natural experiences that Berger and Gilkey do. Those two men are asserting a way to *see* life and the world. It makes most sense, they say, if you suppose that our sense of finitude, our joy and our fear, our whole constellation of life and place is up against something supernatural. As Gilkey puts it:

God, who transcends the secular, can yet be said to be appre-hended in the secular in the sense that every significant joy and every compelling anxiety of ordinary existence reflect an appre-hension of this dimension of the unconditioned, and the aware-ness of his presence or absence.[45]

It is simply and clearly the case that not everyone *sees* that way, although they are looking at the same world. They can-not be dismissed as unaware or immature. There may be an impasse. Thomas Kuhn said that in a conflict of paradigms it is generally the young and those new to the field who affirm the new paradigm. Perhaps there is no choice but to wait and let the proponents of each paradigm, or, in this case, each world view, try to account for as much of the evidence as is available. It clearly is the case that each proponent assumes his own view of things and then argues out of that perspective—to someone doing the same thing from another perspective. Both the theist and the nontheist are able, it seems to me, to account for nearly everything. They live in the same world and are looking at the same things. But they *see* differently.

Leslie Dewart has argued that the confusion exists because of the character of our language. Indo-European languages, he says, are the cause for our inability to speak clearly about God.[46] Greek, Latin, and most of the languages of Western European civilization place a heavy burden on the verb *to be*. In effect, the languages of the Christian tradition tend to reduce all statements to being or not being. Other languages often distinguish, sometimes radically, between being and being something. For us, Dewart says, every complete thought is reducible to the logical form S *is* P. "In other words, the direct implication of the basic syntactic structure of Greek and Latin is that all reality is reducible to being: reality is *that-which-is* and anything whatever which is thinkable is, of course, being: for it is *something-that-is*."[47]

Dewart uses Arabic to illustrate the way in which some languages distinguish between what *is* and what *exists before us*. (He says Chinese does the same thing. I will take his word for it, in both cases.) An Arab, Dewart says, distinguishes between what a thing is and the fact that it may (or may not) stand in the world in front of us, ready to be found. Much later in his argument, Dewart calls this the difference between something that is a reality and something that exists. Reality is knowable (that is the nature of it), but it does not necessarily exist in the world. To put it another way, one can understand realities that exist nowhere. " 'I can *know* what a man or a phoenix is and still be *ignorant* whether it exists in reality.' "[48] To use more contemporary language: the world of existences, of being, of things that are *there*, is the world of fact. "It is *there*, it is a *fact*. Anything that is, is essentially, and as such, a fact."[49]

The root of our difficulty, as Dewart sees it, is that our languages (or at least those languages related to the one I am using here) force us to speak of God quite as we speak of facts. God isn't something that exists as other things exist. But when we say that, the habits of our language and mind lead us to conclude that therefore God doesn't exist, and if God does not exist, God is nothing at all. Neither are we forced to conclude, to save God from nonexistence, that he is a super-being.

It does *not* mean this: that since God in some real sense be a being because otherwise he would be nothing, we must *both* affirm and deny being of him, so that the proposition "God is not a being" really means "God is a super-being." What it means is literally what it says, that God is not a being at all. What the religious experience of God discloses is a reality *beyond* being.[50]

God is not a fact, not an object, does not exist, but he is real and he is present and knowable, Dewart says.

The typically disaffiliated religious person today, Dewart maintains, rejects precisely the kind of absolute theism that makes the person of God an existing someone. So he concludes that God is a force. And that, Dewart believes, is a mistake but an understandable one. It led to radical disbelief, in stages. The first stage was agnosticism. The existence of God could not be proved, but neither could it be disproved. Skepticism was reasonable. The second stage was antitheism: "Anti-theism issued from agnosticism out of the realization that religious belief in a God whose existence was problematic was not a harmless anodyne, but a disease of human consciousness."[51] And the third stage is Christian disbelief, resulting in several varieties of atheism.

Contemporary thought is perfectly consistent. Its atheistic conclusion is formally materially valid on its own premises, and there is no question of attempting to catch its logical mistake. The traditional Christian concept is simply not viable. . . . It is probably only a matter of time . . . before the point becomes self-evident to almost everyone.[52]

The error lies in thinking of God as being at all: God is reality, Dewart says. Much of the problem of contemporary belief will disappear when we learn to make that distinction.

I suggest that in the future we may not feel the need to conceive God as a super-natural being. If we discard the hellenic view of nature, the Christian God no longer must, in order to remain free, gracious and freely self-giving, perform super-natural feats, under-take super-natural functions and roles, or enjoy super-natural status.[53]

"Religious experience, then, does not reveal a transcendent being: what it reveals is that being exists in the presence of a reality which transcends it."[54]

Dewart's argument is a curious one. Our problem (we Western men), he says, is that "we tend to identify the way in which *we* in this tradition think, with the way in which *man* thinks."[55] Dewart, on the other hand, seems to believe that reality corresponds to the way Arabs and Chinese think. He agrees that the way we think cannot support a God concept. But if we could believe that reality and existence are not neces-sarily identical, we could call God a reality, and everything would be all right. But that sounds peculiarly like saying if there were elves we could believe in elves. There are people who do believe in elves. Some of us don't. Language isn't just a tool, an interchangeable tool, language is the symbolic rep-resentation of a way of seeing the world. When Dewart pro-poses that we can modify our language and make room for God, he is begging the question. The problem is not simply that we cannot find any existing object or person called God, although that is true. Dewart admits that we simply cannot imagine a superbeing called God, either. On the face of it, imagining a superbeing called God does not seem to be awfully much more difficult than imagining a reality who does not exist called God. In both cases we are asked to think that some other kind of nature, or reality, or being, lies alongside our existence. It is because we find that impossible that our lan-guage is as it is. Of course if we saw things differently we would see things differently, and we would talk differently, too. The problem of God is not appreciably altered by denying existence to that other reality. Dewart simply proposes that that other reality is not quite as we thought it was, and if we could learn to think differently we could believe differently.

That is true. But we don't see the world that way. World views are not so arbitrarily exchanged.

What is the strength of theism?

"Life," George Santayana said, "is a spontaneous, crude,

ignorant ambition: a blind self-assertion big with every sort of self-contradiction, agony, and crime. It is precisely that from which a veritable religion would come to redeem us."[56] Santayana thinks "we are prone to imagine a God, more powerful and more friendly than our human neighbors, more powerful and friendly even than the ordinary course of nature, who shall abet us in our hazardous enterprise and assure us of ultimate success."[57] Santayana understands man to be in a precarious position in the world. We didn't choose life. It happened to us. We live, but we are powerless to live. It is as if we were in the hands of an alien and inscrutable power, hostile and unfathomable. Gilkey talks like that, too, and in an obtuse way so does Berger. Death is very large for all of them. Gilkey capitalizes "Void" but not "life." That is a common human feeling. As Santayana says, it comes upon a man "in the night, in the desert, when he finds himself, as the Arabs say, alone with Allah."[58]

There is another side to theism. Life is not only a balancing act on the edge of an abyss. There is awe and wonder, and laughter and lovemaking, and puzzlement, and dreams, and a thousand things that make us reluctant to end the day and anxious to begin the next early. There is even the chance that, whatever is now the fact, it might become something new. "To love things as they are would be a mockery of things: a true lover must love them as they would wish to be."[59] Those kinds of things move us, too, no less than the void. They have power.

And . . . when power takes on the form of life, and begins to circle about and pursue some type of perfection, spirit in us necessarily loves these perfections, since spirit is aspiration become conscious, and they are the goals of life: and in so far as any of these goals of life can be defined or attained anywhere, even if only in prophetic fancy, they become glory, or become beauty, and spirit in us necessarily worships them: not only the troubled glories and brief perfections of this world only, but rather that desired perfection, that eternal beauty, which lies sealed in the heart of each living thing.[60]

God.

That kind of thing cannot be impersonal. God like that isn't a cause or a force. Theism is an insistence on something about person, personhood, personal involvement. Life isn't a transaction, a process, a production. It is about flesh and blood, about life, about fear, about affection, about *me*. I matter, and life matters. I care and am cared for. Theism assures that. John Robinson knows that. Life, he says, is a Thou, and he is made someone—an *I*—by his confrontation with life. But how does one say that? John Robinson and generations of Christians have said that the universe, or something at the heart of the existence—God—is personal, and knowing that makes us someone, someone worth caring for and cared for. God cares. Jacques Monod says the universe is alien and cold, and perhaps it is. But the universe is also our mother, who has given birth to such as we. The question is whether we can affirm what we profoundly feel and think about ourselves and the world—that we want to care for it and each other—without having to imagine someone super who watches us.

Maybe someone is watching us, who created us in his image. Maybe. Some people do see the world that way. I think I know what they mean.

CHAPTER 6

On Getting
Sea Legs

I used to go to sea. It was hard to get used to walking on an unpredictable deck. It was almost as hard to control one's legs as one's stomach. It happened, sometimes, that a sea lion would discover that we were doing half his work for him, and he would patiently strip our lines clean of every fish and then, with a satisfied roar, surface and eat just the liver. It takes a lot of liver to satisfy a ton of sea lion. Although other less understanding law codes did not permit it, the law of survival stipulated that I might get out a high-powered rifle and shoot at the sea lion. It is very hard to hit a sea lion that is going up and down and sideways from the deck of a small boat that is going down and sideways and up. Sometimes I missed the sea lion by a generous half mile. Sometimes I was lucky and the sound of the rifle scared him away. In every case the gun rusted a little more.

It was there I learned relativity.

It was bad enough that the Polish astronomer Copernicus rearranged the universe, or, if he did not rearrange it, that he at least proposed to see everything differently. So far as we know, the universe itself did not appreciably change as a

126

result of what Copernicus said, but the way people thought about it did change. Before Copernicus, we at least knew where we were: we were the center of creation, surrounded by glory of every kind, right where God wanted us to be. We had a universe, an orderly and splendid arrangement of things around us.

Copernicus had the good sense to die the year his major work was published. It probably saved him a lot of trouble. It is a grievous crime to deprive man of his privileged seat at the center of the cosmos. Galileo discovered *that* when he endorsed Copernicus' views and even added to the evidence. He was tried and sentenced to life imprisonment (house arrest, as it turned out), and his works were banned. It is a terrible thing to hear that the earth, created for man, is a very small place, rather on the edge of things, no one knows precisely just where. We are wandering. Earth is a very small place, about the size of a quarter, when seen from halfway to the moon. Pascal described our human reactions to that knowledge even better than the National Aeronautics and Space Administration (one might have guessed that):

When I consider the short duration of my life, swallowed up in the eternity before and after, the little space which I fill, and even can see, engulfed in the infinite immensity of spaces of which I am ignorant and which knew me not, I am frightened, and am astonished at being here rather than there; . . . why now rather than then. Who has put me here? By whose order and direction have this place and this time been allotted to me? The eternal silence of these infinite spaces frightens me.[1]

It is not just the large and silent spaces that matter. It is to know the blind and independent nature of the universe. It is to know that, although Newton tried valiantly to hold on to his religion, there was nothing there for God to do. And there is no center. There is no mooring point. Everything gets along without a center. And that may be the problem. "There is no center though a center really ought to be."[2]

Newton built a mechanical universe for which God, as Nietzsche expressed it, was far too extreme a hypothesis,[3] in which stars and planets, men and animals, particles of matter and particles of light (as it was thought) moved regularly, inexorably in accord with mathematical laws. Newton ordered time and space. "Absolute, true, and mathematical time," Newton said, "of itself and from its own nature, flows equably, without relation to anything external, and by another name is called duration." Space could be "absolute space, in its own nature, without relation to anything external," which "remains always similar and immovable," or it could be relative space, which was "some movable dimension or measure of the absolute spaces."[4] The details are not important here, but it clearly followed from Newtonian physics that the mechanical laws of the universe, which we observe and depend on every day, apply equally to objects whether moving or at rest. Measurements made in one situation are valid in the other. So, although a Copernican and Newtonian world dwarfed man and consigned him to a lost and silent corner, at least it was regular. One knew what to depend on, how to measure.

Early in this century another Pole exclaimed, "A new Copernicus is born! Read Einstein's paper."[5] Einstein had shown in his Special Theory of Relativity that there was no appropriate place for absolutes when motion was considered. If, for instance, I assert that a measuring rod shrinks as its speed increases, or that a clock slows toward a standstill as it approaches the speed of light, relative to a stationary observer but *not* to one moving with the measure or the clock, then the import of Einstein's assertions starts to become clear. Time and space aren't absolutes. They are relative to the position of the observer. Whereas the Special Theory applied to bodies in uniform motion, Einstein's General Theory demonstrated that gravity was a function of matter and that what *looks* straight to us is really a curve. The laws of Euclidean geometry, which every schoolchild learns, are only a workable approximation on a small scale of something far more sophisticated. A straight line is not always the shortest distance between two points. Most of us who deal with time and space in crude and rough-hand ways are perfectly safe in assuming that straight lines are straight lines and that an hour is an hour everywhere because it works well enough. As Mrs. Einstein replied when asked if she understood the theory, "Oh, no, although he has explained it to me so many times—but it is not necessary to my happiness."[6] Happiness aside, time and space, as eternally silent as they were for Pascal, are not even what they seem to be. When asked if he could explain relativity in a few sentences, Einstein provided a classic answer:

If you will not take the answer too seriously, only as a kind of joke, then I can explain it as follows. It was formerly believed that if all material things disappeared out of the universe, time and space would be left. According to the relativity theory, however, time and space disappear together with the things.[7]

Or to put it in more personal terms, Einstein demonstrated that time and space are not just there, plain to see, measure, and record. What we see is dependent on where we are and how we are measuring. It depends. "Modern science looks at nature from the viewpoint of a man, not from that of an angel."[8]

And there are no angelic points of view. It *all* depends.

It was not only in the physical sciences that absolutes began to waver, although one can point there to names like Copernicus, Newton, Lavoisier, Planck, Einstein, and Heisenberg. The Darwinian revolution in the middle of the last century may be the most fundamental intellectual event in man's history. If it is, it is because the idea of evolution, almost from the very beginning, applied not only to the world around man but to man himself. Before Darwin's age, it was generally believed that everything in nature was planned, designed, and had a predetermined end. Even now, more than a century later, the theologians of hope and futurity are still flirting with the belief that history is going somewhere already determined. They are fairly sophisticated about it, but it is the same general notion. Even when the great age of the earth began to become evident, and when fossils of animals no longer extant were found, still the belief in fixed and unchangeable species was maintained.

Ernst Mayr argues that the biological revolution has been so reluctantly accepted because it involved a change in world views.[9] He distinguishes a whole constellation of elements involved in the change from a static to a developmental view of life in the world. The age of the earth had to be radically reconsidered. Geology and paleontology forced scientists to abandon a recent (6,000 years ago) origin for the earth. Both catastrophism and a steady-state view of the earth had to be rejected. In an effort to account for the extinction of certain species, and what seemed to be clear breaks between successive geological and biological epochs, it had generally been believed that the earth had been subject to a whole series of creations and destructions—thirty, fifty, or even more than a hundred. In opposition to that, Charles Lyell had promoted a steady-state concept of the world, in which the creator constantly intervened to maintain general uniformity or in which natural laws produced the same effect. Proponents of evolution maintained, in contrast, that the world and life on it was steadily changing. In the third place, those who had proposed evolution even before Darwin had argued that such change as was evident progressively moved toward perfection. That was only a modification of the argument that the earth as a special creation of God was perfect (at least at the beginning, before having been spoiled). Darwin concluded that change was not always for the better. Even today that is not generally recognized outside the scientific community, even by those who affirm evolution. The generations of life, victims of chance, try things: everything.

The replicative system, far from being able to eliminate the microscopic perturbations by which it is invariably beset, knows only how to register and offer them—almost always in vain—to the teleonomic filter by which their performance is finally judged, through natural selection.[10]

That is to say, life produces quirks; a few are advantageous for survival; most are not. Fourth, Mayr says, the acceptance of biological evolution entailed the rejection of creationism. Every antievolutionary position prior to Darwin assumed either the intermittent or the constant personal interference of the Creator. To propose that the process itself could account for its own changes was, in effect, to eliminate the necessity for a Creator at all. Evolution also shifted the focus of attention from the essences of things to the importance of populations, although that may be the slowest shift to be recognized.

And finally, the acceptance of evolutionary thinking, Mayr proposes, abolishes anthropocentrism. Man became one of the animals, however carefully Darwin skirted the issue with *The Origin of Species.*

The biological revolution is just that, a revolution. At least as dramatically as the Copernican revolution or the assertion of relativity by Einstein or the uncertainty principle by Heisenberg, it has involved an enormous relocation of our perspective on ourselves. As late as the writing of this material, the school systems of California and Tennessee are still trying to decide whether to teach the evolution of life to students. Hermann J. Muller said in 1959 that one hundred years without Darwin are enough, but it appears now it may take longer. The acceptance of biological evolution entails a whole complex of viewpoints which, when bundled together, constitutes a veritable world view. Man is not necessary. He is contingent. We would like to think that we are necessary, inevitable, even ordained from eternity, but it is not so. We are here, and that is an astonishment and a delight, but it could have been otherwise, and if we do not take care it will be otherwise.

Ever since its birth in the Ionian Islands almost three thousand years ago, Western philosophy has been divided between two seemingly opposed attitudes. According to one of them the authentic and ultimate truth of the world can reside only in perfectly immutable forms, by essence unvarying. According to the other, the only real truth resides in flux and evolution.[11]

It is the claim to relativity, in contrast to anything absolute, that the sciences have pressed upon us, biology perhaps most profoundly in terms of our own apprehension of ourselves, although it is physics that has given us a name for relativity. But relativity, or perhaps better for these purposes, relativism,[12] is not impressed on us only from the basic sciences. Peter Berger, who is himself a sociologist, argues persuasively that the social sciences pose even more critical challenges for theology. Sociology is preceded by both history and psychology, and a convincing argument might be offered that it was nineteenth-century historical scholarship that first recognized the human and temporal character of those literary sources

that had been invested with almost divine worth: the scriptures. Even more, beyond having established the sources—
the human sources—of biblical materials, historians specified
the ways in which those materials were both written and interpreted relative to the situation of those who dealt with them.
"Put simply, historical scholarship led to a perspective in
which even the most sacrosanct elements of religious tradition
came to be seen as human products."[13] I have already suggested the way in which psychology after Freud uncovered
the last hiding place for God: in feeling. Friedrich Schleiermacher was the last major theologian entitled to think it might
be God who occasions feelings within us of absolute dependence or awe or anything else. Freud, and psychology ever
since, regularly reminds us of the unmistakably human origins
of dreams and visions—even dreams and visions of God—
and of every notion and exercise that ever inhabited the human
mind. We think and feel things that are apparently so, as well
as things that are patently not so. But whether or not, after
having sorted them out, we determine they are reliable, we
know they belong to us. For that reason we arrest people who
believe they have had a command from God to set fire to the
church on the corner, and we wonder uneasily even about the
zealot who claims to have received less damaging information
from the Almighty. (If the newspaper reports from South
Africa are accurate, Billy Graham, who talks to God, thinks
the death penalty will stop people from killing each other and
proposes that rapists ought to be castrated. That is a powerful
but probably unintended argument on behalf of restricting
Supreme Court seats to infidels.)

Berger argues that, even more than history and psychology,
sociology has intensified the crisis.

The historical nature and product-character, and thus the relativity rather than absolutism, of the religious traditions become
even more transparent as the social dynamics of their historical
production is understood. And the notion of projection becomes
much more plausible in its sociological rather than its psychological form, because the former is simpler and more readily
verifiable in ordinary, "conscious" experience.[14]

Precisely because we cannot unerringly depend on our sense experience, we have to rely on social support for our conceptions of what is real, and what societies can and will believe duplicates nearly the whole range of individual human experience.[15]

"Reality" is socially constructed. Just as there is neither time nor space without material things, so is there no "reality" without a society. The fact that what the world means, and the way it is organized, has social origins also means that entrance into its patterns and attitudes is automatic and unexamined. We are born into a society and learn the symbolic system of the society in such a way that cultural patterns and values have a coercive effect on us. Language does more than provide symbols for eating and singing and quarreling. "Language . . . constructs immense edifices of symbolic representations that appear to tower over the reality of everyday life like gigantic presences from another world."[16] To speak that way does not mean that language, any particular language, simply leaps full-grown into existence. Language is symbol reflecting the world view or, less grandly, the attitudes and commitments of the people who mold their language. But for the child, or for the cultural immigrant, the language, reflecting a whole constellation of attitudes, values, commitments, and perspectives, is simply *there*. Learning to use a particular language, whether for a child or for an adult, is more than mastering grammar and vocabulary. It is to learn to *think* in a certain way. Language forces a kind of reality on us, a reality shaped (even if unconsciously) by the society that uses that symbolic structure.

In the same way, when a society has evolved highly abstracted language patterns to refer to its cultural institutions, whether religion, philosophy, art, or science, the language itself, already carrying the full weight of the cultural approval, presents those patterns as if they were objective realities. But however massive and matter-of-fact that institutional world is, however confidently and clearly the language assumes those institutional patterns, they are humanly produced. "Society is a human product. Society is an objective reality. Man is a social product."[17] The patterns of a society, then, come to us as if they were larger than life. "Reification is the apprehension of human phenomena as if they were things, that is, in non-human or possibly supra-human terms."[18] Reified social realities may be considered to be self-evident facts of nature, or eternal cosmic laws, or manifestations of divine will. Reification demonstrates that men are capable of, and even prone to, forgetting their own authorship of the human world. Social institutions and cultural attitudes are then regarded as powerful and objective *facts* to which the wise man will conform. The result is that the human beings who created the world of meaning and institutions around them begin to regard themselves as subject to those inexorable "facts." "Typically," then, in that situation, "the real relationship between man and his world is reversed in consciousness. Man, the producer of a world, is apprehended as its product, and human activity as an epiphenomenon of non-human processes."[19] People, in other words, produce realities that deny them. Marriage, for instance, may be regarded as divinely commanded, as a natural law, as a necessary consequence of certain biological or psychological forces, or even as a necessary component of a viable social system. What is common to all of these reifications is that marriage *as a human product* has been obscured. It becomes necessity and fate, to be lived through happily or unhappily.[20]

The correspondence between what sociologists call reification on the level of a society and what Ludwig Feuerbach called projection on the level of the individual is plain. Feuerbach was concerned not with social structures as such but with the way humans reify their more personal value systems. He said that, in effect, we distill from the whole of human behavior those characteristics we affirm and project them outside ourselves. Then, having done that, we invest them with a reality of their own and, forgetting they are our objects, make them subjects, or a Subject, who then treats us like objects. Or better, we conduct ourselves as objects before the Subject we have created. Insofar, then, as marriage (to use that example) is regarded as God's command, we actually have one reification commanding another reification to human beings who have forgotten what they have wrought.

It is the sociologist who attempts to discover and record the particular history of social behavior. If the sociologist does his job well, it becomes evident that what at first seemed to be absolute patterns of human behavior are human creations. But insofar as we learn that it is we who have constructed what we had regarded as the objective framework of reality, we become faced with precisely the dilemma the social reality was intended to overcome: chaos. "*All* social reality is precarious. *All* societies are constructions in the face of chaos."[21] It may not be true; I do not believe it is true; but it is widely held that, as Dostoevski put it in *The Brothers Karamazov*, "If God does not exist, all things are permitted." And that is chaos. It was against chaos that the reality was constructed, and it was against chaos that social and personal realities were invested with absolute authority. To the extent that a people believes that a world without absolutes is a chaotic world, to the extent that they believe that the absence of God permits everything, then chaos threatens them. It is for that reason, I think, that even people who have come to realize that God is functionally dormant in their lives nevertheless refuse to refute him. Chaos cannot be permitted. Only a fool would prefer that. And it is for that reason, too, that the symbol God is intimately bound up with meaning and order and purpose and value on the *largest* scale. It is an affirmation in the face of the largest conceivable kind of chaos that *all* reality is, finally, good and meaningful.[22]

Everywhere we look, everything we think about, the stars and ideas alike, suggest that nothing is absolute.

The resultant sense of the relativity of all things in the passage of time—of the forms of the cosmos itself, of natural life, of our own species, of political and social structures, of the most significant historical events, the noblest of ideas, the most sacred of scriptures, institutions or creeds—practically defines our era.[23]

What is the significance of anything we do, of everything we do, if everything is relative? *Can* there be significance? Can one live with relativism?

"Does it frighten us," Karl Barth asked, "to discover how completely all that we are and do moves within the sphere of relativity? Perhaps it does, but this is precisely what we must discover."[24]

"I accept the universe," said Margaret Fuller.
"By God, you'd better!" retorted Thomas Carlyle.[25]

"To reaffirm the same old faith in a louder voice helps very little; it only gives further evidence of our deep anxieties."[26]

Karl Barth was able to look relativity right in the eye without flinching because he proceeded from a profoundly pessimistic assessment of man. He affirmed relativity because he believed that all human knowledge was both relative and futile. He excepted his knowledge of God from the general rule and turned, then, to God for an absolute way out of the dilemma. But if God is our own creation, in effect a world view, Barth's solution is no solution at all, but a delusion.

It is extremely difficult to bridge the gulf between trying to accept what seems an inescapably relative world and the need for some kind of certainty. The difficulty can be illustrated by the way in which Peter Berger himself, who is not only a fine sociologist but also a theologian of no mean stature, attempts to deal with the dilemma. After affirming relativism, or relativity, he concludes that since all opinions and positions are relative, he is free to affirm a position that is no longer in vogue. So he assumes there is a supernatural reality. That is to say, he assumes something that is *not* relative: God.[27]

The opponents of relativism charge that relativism is a philosophical position that can be demonstrated to be logically contradictory. The advocates of relativism generally attempt to show that men do in fact think and value differently, and they conclude, from that nearly indisputable fact, that thought and values are relative to the particular situation. But to assert that as a philosophical or logical position, opponents say, is to make everything except that assertion relative: it alone is absolute. But that is to fail to recognize the two levels on which that debate is waged. The relativist is not so much proposing a philosophical truth as he is describing a way of proceeding, a way of proceeding that, if it is done well, does not forget that all positions and opinions, even those one elects to trust and to act on, however satisfying, are not absolute. I think one can do that.

"By God, you'd better!" retorted Thomas Carlyle.

One cannot appeal to "facts" to settle the differences between the way people see the world. The facts themselves are functions of the point of view from which they are apprehended.[28] As Thomas Kuhn showed with reference to paradigm conflict, the debate is necessarily circular. Each one uses his own understanding of the way things really are to argue on behalf of his own paradigm. It *must* be that way. It would be a kind of intellectual suicide to assume what appears to be an erroneous position to defend something else, a little like arguing that God makes atheism necessary. Only with sarcasm can that be said. Circular arguments finally depend on persuasion, on the appeal inherent in the demonstration of how well the position accounts for things. That is the only force, too, of the relativistic position.

It is, I said earlier, probably a function of our own intelligence that we drive toward coherence, toward an overview of things. It is a way of living with what otherwise is chaos. Even when we know that we have no right to claim to have found the absolute truth, nevertheless we do such ordering and sorting and evaluating as we can. Kaufman says that

we eventually arrive at a set of basic convictions—or first principles or self-evident truths or innate ideas or absolute presuppositions—which appear to be self-justifying and in terms of which we always find that we are justifying and explicating all other truth.[29]

Those convictions, principles, truths, or whatever one happens to name them are not accorded genuinely absolute status. They are a way to proceed. They are the farthest limit to which we, at the moment, can find validity, and we find them fruitful ways of ordering other ideas. T. Z. Lavine calls them "functional absolutes,"[30] but that is an unhappy choice of names because of the way it perpetuates absolutes precisely where that is not intended. But what is more important is that the relativity of our knowledge does not destroy our norms and lead into nihilism. Neither does it presuppose that we have found absolute norms. "It simply involves the acknowledgment that the norms under which we stand are normative for us and inescapable for us, but this is understood as not necessarily implying that they are normative for everyone in every situation."[31] We never escape relativity.

We try often enough. The affirmation of relativism with respect to God-language is doubly difficult because in part the term God functions precisely to deny relativism, or at least to affirm something absolute. For that reason, people who cannot conceive of reality any other way will fight like tigers to defend the uniqueness of God. The question, of course, is whether in that instance a "functional absolute" has been "reified" (to use the sociological term); whether it is a human projection invested with ontological status (Feuerbach). It is important to note that, in cases where some affirm God as a "functional absolute" and others affirm God's absolute status, both groups will live and act in the same ways. Particularly in the situation where both groups use the term God to refer to something like love, it might seem to border on insanity to let blood over the issue. In both cases that would be a denial of their best commitment. It is moral self-mutilation.

As conditions change, as situations change, our affirmations and our convictions, our vision and our world views change. That is to be expected logically and is amply demonstrated historically and sociologically; "no truth which anyone has ever known has been absolute, though it may very well have been valid for its time, its historical situation."[32] A look around at the world, past and present, suggests that everyone must stand where he is, in a situation that raises certain problems and offers certain possibilities, and learn as much as possible from analogous situations. To the extent that situations are similar, a good deal can be borrowed and affirmed, but to the degree to which ones' own situation is particular, modifications must be made, new configurations must be supposed, and some earlier "truths" probably ought to be denied. At the same time it must be remembered that the future will similarly look back at our best constructions of "reality." Above all, physics, biology, psychology, history, and sociology ought to teach modesty. We do not overcome relativity. "Nevertheless, we can continue to work and to live and to think as finite, historical beings without falling into despair, because we find our working and living and thinking to be *meaningful* for us in our present experience."[33]

That is very hard to learn. A good case can be made that despair over the loss of absolutes, apprehended as surrender to chaos, is what defines the contemporary mind. The editors of *The Discontinuous Universe*, a volume of writings from about forty well-known thinkers of fairly recent time, suggest that around 1850 (roughly Darwin's era) something happened to human consciousness "as the assumption that we lived in a coherent, ordered universe began to break down and, with it, the bourgeois values that had been dependent on it."[34] All the structures humans had evolved in order to make the world intelligible seem more metaphoric than anything else, "interesting, effective, even magical perhaps, but arbitrary, interchangeable, with their ideal aim of corresponding to structures that 'really' exist in the universe forever unverifiable."[35] Instead reality seems ambiguously, disturbingly, even self-destructively in flux. In response the artist has attempted to find a place for indeterminacy and chaos within his art, whether that be the unconscious sources of imagery in surrealism, the chance paintings of Jackson Pollock, the use of random numbers in dance, poetry, and painting, the random sounds and rhythms in John Cage's music, the planned chaos of "happenings" in theater, or the provocation of the audience into anger and unpredictable action. "Madness itself," the editors write, "becomes a decisive symbol for modern consciousness."[36]

The ease with which Christianity appropriated Platonic or neo-Platonic categories is nowhere more striking than at the point where the church is confronted with radical, imprecise change. Church members regularly display the stoutest kind of resistance even to what, on the face of it, seems to be trivial change. God help the unwitting clergyman who wants to remove that awful picture of Jesus from over the altar where it has hung for years, or who has the tenacious courage to assign unfamiliar hymns, or who perhaps simply reads the scriptures from any version of the Bible subsequent to about 1611! There is a Platonist somewhere inside most church members who regularly whispers that real things, true things, are unchanging things. It is, I think, because we tend to identify the truth with permanence; the truth remains forever. And if God is truth, the finest and most durable of all truths, God must necessarily be the most permanent of all permanent things. So church members come to worship with the inarticulated assumption somewhere deep down that worship is a way to touch enduring things, permanent things, forever things. They refuse to sing new hymns and vote to keep the picture over the altar.

Neither is it an accident that the theologians of hope and future (a name so full of tomorrow, so burdened with yesterday) seize upon first-century Christian eschatology. The promise of a certain victory, of a glorious future, has always sustained a people threatened with chaos. Whatever else is to be said for the current theological scene, it is not notably confident of what it is doing. The hope-and-future theologians are, for the most part, the academic children of Karl Barth and Paul Tillich. With Karl Barth they have very little confidence in the ability of human beings to do much about the human situation. Although they know that much of the rest of Barthian theology is gone, that much remains. And with Paul Tillich they display considerable confidence that they are dealing with some kind of ultimate truth. They believe that the absolute future has begun to reveal itself in the midst of our chaos, and sometimes they speak with scorn about theologians who, like paupers, have nothing to offer but "human" hopes, as if they themselves held the secrets of the universe in their hands. It is worth remembering that even theologians of the eschatological variety are mortal men, that their ideas are only human ideas, and that, so far as the last century has had anything at all to teach, it has taught us to be modest, if not even suspicious, about absolute truth. The theologians of hope and future have seen the future, all right, and it is here, and it frightens them.

Manfred Hoffman says that the gradual process of secularization which characterizes the West at present is precisely an increasing emancipation from absolute, metahistorical authorities. He writes:

The pronouncement of the death of God must be interpreted as expressing the experience of the loss of any type of unifying principle beyond man or in man that could be used as a criterion for understanding himself and the world as a whole.[37]

The utter relativity of human existence, he says, forces the theologian to forsake any claim to an absolute outside of, or within, man. Hoffmann, like the hope theologians, thinks that the eschatological future is the place for absolutes, and that is probably a kind of backhanded recognition that there are none here. The eschatological affirmation today is a retreat into precisely that absolute domain which a century of scholarship and human experience has repudiated.

Peter Berger manages to repudiate his absolutes and have them too by arguing that, since all ideas are relative, and theoretically, then, sometimes permissable too, he will affirm a currently unpopular position. He finds virtue in being in a cognitive minority. In the name of pervasive relativity he defends his supernatural absolute: God. That is a good trick if you can do it, but it is a trick, nonetheless.

Even Alistair Kee, who sets out with fierce determination to live in the twentieth-century world, finally cannot come to terms with a relative world. He does not want to talk about God—as has been said, the subtitle of his book is *Christian Faith Without Belief in God*—but he clearly intends not only to talk about absolutes but to *insist* on at least one.

Kee is concerned to translate talk about God into *something*, not simply to eliminate it, as nineteenth-century biblical theology tended to do with passages it could not accept. He cites Karl Barth with approbation:

My reply is that if I have a system, it is limited to recognition of what Kierkegaard called the "infinite qualitative distinction" between time and eternity, and to my regarding this as possessing negative as well as positive significance: "God is in heaven, and thou art on earth."[38]

"What seems to be central to theology," Kee responds, "is the 'infinite qualitative distinction.' "

It is not clear why Kee believes that the "infinite qualitative distinction" is of the very essence of what people mean when they say God, but he does think it is so. While, then, he is ready to abandon theism, he chooses to retain the "distinction." He is not happy about the word "infinite" but, were he to suggest another, he would choose "absolute" or "ultimate."[39] Kee does not think that the word God, or any other term intending to stand in its place, can refer simply to something mundane. The idea of a personal God must go, he says, but the infinite qualitative distinction must be retained. "If the distinction— yet to be analysed—is eliminated, then there would seem to be no point in retaining the word 'God' at all. Should the distinction go, then there really would be no theology."[40] In the past the distinction was expressed in terms of either the supernatural or the metaphysical, but today, Kee says, those categories carry too many traditional meanings he does not intend. He suggests that the early Hebrew view of God represented the distinction in terms of power. God was the reality who was an insurmountable obstacle to men bent on pursuing their own ends and, alternately, a never-failing source of power in the pursuit of quite different ends (ends not specified by Kee).

Kee suggests that "the way of transcendence" is a term adequate to indicate what people have meant when they said God. Jesus is definitive for the Christian precisely in that in him the way of transcendence is realized in flesh and blood. "We point to Jesus and say 'God is like that.' Or in the terminology we have been developing, we might say 'Jesus is the very incarnation of the way of transcendence.' "[41] Kee had earlier defined the Christian faith as "commitment with ultimate concern to that which came to expression in Jesus Christ."[42] Jesus Christ is the incarnation of transcendence, "understood quite literally." "When 'God' is what theology is about, then Jesus Christ is quite literally the incarnation of God."[43]

The alternative to the way of transcendence is the way of immanence. The division in society, Kee says, is precisely between those who are committed to transcendence and those committed to immanence. The way of immanence is a commitment to the "natural" life. "The biblical phrase 'the world,' intended in the pejorative sense of being 'that which is opposed to God,' can be used here. In this context we can say that the 'way of immanence' represents the natural 'way of the world.'"[44] Nietzsche, for whom Kee has many good things to say, erred precisely at the point where he focused attention on the natural life for man, Kee says. Nietzsche saw that Christianity was an alternative to natural man. Even though Kee thinks Nietzsche made the wrong choice, Kee concedes Nietzsche did recognize the "infinite qualitative distinction" between the way of transcendence and the way of immanence.

"In choosing the way of transcendence, we make a value judgment that things are not as they seem. We are disputing reality."[45] People other than Christians are also committed to the way of transcendence, but what distinguishes the Christian is the claim that Jesus Christ is "the very embodiment and final revelation of the way of transcendence."[46] The way of the cross is not "the natural way," Kee says; the natural way must be negated before we can accept this new way of transcendence.

In spite of his repeated assertions that one must choose between them, it is simply not clear what Kee intends to distinguish with his two "ways." He plainly says that contemporary men cannot believe in two kinds of reality, but at the same time he insists that there is an "infinite qualitative distinction" between the way of Jesus and the natural ways of the world. With Nietzsche he agrees that man must be surpassed, but Kee thinks that Nietzsche could not accomplish that because he affirmed the natural way of man. It does not clarify things at all when he says, "We test out our suspicion that the 'real' nature of man is (to put it in summary fashion) embodied in Jesus Christ, and not a Nazi Führer."[47] Unless Kee has another reality up his sleeve somewhere, which he says is not the case, it would seem to make much more sense simply to contrast Jesus with alternate embodiments of ways to be in the world. To introduce "transcendence" as a designation for one particular way of living and thinking might seem only to confuse the issue. Why is the way of Jesus Christ, "the way of transcendence," not as natural as Nietzsche's way, or even the Führer's way? Nietzsche's way may dissatisfy us, and the Führer's way may dismay us, but what is so unnatural about them? Both ways are neither more nor less human than Jesus' way, although they may be more common. Does Kee simply mean that Jesus' way is a better way, an "infinitely" better way, a way that is so superior that it "transcends" all other "natural" ways? Why should that constitute an "infinite qualitative distinction"? Kee himself admits that Christians are not distinguished by *that* commitment. Christians are distinguished by affirming Jesus as the embodiment and final revelation of the way of transcendence.[48] If "transcendence" is not peculiar to Christians, or to Jesus, why does he not just say that, more than any other person, Jesus embodies (or incarnates) that better (or even best) way, and we affirm him? If the transcendent way is found apart from Jesus and Christians, it would seem to follow that the most one might claim is that Jesus is relatively better than other instances of the transcendent way. And that is *not* an "infinite qualitative distinction."

Alistair Kee proposes to abandon God-language because God is part of a belief system (or world view) we cannot any longer affirm. But he speaks of absolutes and ultimates as easily as Paul Tillich did, using precisely Tillich's categories, in fact. Jesus Christ is "infinitely, qualitatively distinct" from natural human ways. Jesus is the "final revelation" of the way of transcendence. Christians are committed "with ultimate concern" to that which came to expression in Jesus Christ. One might say "absolute" or "ultimate" instead of "infinite"; that is what he means. God, or the way of transcendence, is not something mundane. "Should the distinction go, then there really would be no theology." Kee does not at all seem to recognize that ultimates and absolutes are just as much a part of a defunct belief system as is the notion of God as a super-person. The distinction between some absolutely true things and some relatively true things cannot any longer be maintained. And if that is the case, one cannot make absolute claims about Jesus either, not absolutely absolute claims. At most one can affirm Jesus as "functionally absolute" (to use Lavine's term). That is to say, recognizing that all commitments, all lives, all conceptions and embodiments of the good and satisfying and freeing life are valid and normative only within bounds and are *not* absolute; recognizing that, we affirm Jesus as the one who, above all others, is valid and normative for *us*. We might refashion our lives because of Jesus, might find liberation and fulfillment and joy in Jesus, might live and die for that commitment. But that Jesus is a *final* revelation and *absolute* way? No. We know too much about the world to say that.

We are much rather in the position of Abraham, who believed that when he got to the promised land something final would be realized, and who discovered that there must be more to come, more to be said. It was less than a final promised rest. We are much rather in the position of those children of Israel who believed that when they escaped from Egypt they would finally attain bliss in a land flowing with milk and honey where God would dwell with them forever, who realized that even the house of David was not forever. We are much more like the exiles who wept for Jerusalem, where they might rebuild their dwelling place with God, who discovered that the glory was gone. We are like those who prayed for the Messiah who would usher in the kingdom of God, where there should be neither tears nor injustice, and who know that even that dream was partial. So like all our fathers before us, we live fully expecting the next event to be the last, ultimate, absolutely conclusive event, "when the Lord comes again." At least we used to think that. Now we know there are no ultimate events, no absolute truths, no last times. We live where we are, conscious of the stream of life, committed to such a life as seems to us best. For the Christian, that life is defined by Jesus more than any other.

It is still not an *absolute* commitment. Religions present us with a vision of life. The visions that religions present us are not all alike because beneath each vision lies an understanding of the human situation, an understanding that shapes the vision.[49] "The religious man . . . sees something differently. What does he see? I think we must say that he sees life differently."[50] One of the ways of distinguishing several apprehensions of the life situation is to isolate what seem to be the principal problems of human life.[51] If, for example, where human life is dependent on grass, sheep, crops, weather, sun, and rain, the world of nature is seen as the dominating fact of life, religion is quite likely to focus on the necessity for harmony with nature, and evil is likely to be understood as a breach of the right relationship to nature. If suffering is understood to be the great human dilemma, then insofar as the suffering is considered to reside in human responsibility, religion might consist in a way to deal with one's own responses to pain and grief and sorrow: perhaps stoicism. "Another possible conception of man's principal problem in life . . . is that it consists in my fellowman, more accurately in my relationships with my fellowmen."[52] In that case the chief obstacle is not in nature, or one's own attitudes toward life, but in one's relationships with others. Sheer nastiness or hardheartedness toward each other may be the problem, and an acute awareness of injustice toward others lies at the root of life seen that way. It is likely to produce a religion focused on personal ethic, emphasizing sin, conscience, and repentance. That view characterizes the Semitic religions: Judaism, Christianity, Islam, and Zoroastrianism. Or life might be seen to consist of utter absurdity, as Camus, Sartre, and Beckett describe it. Insofar as religion responds to that, as some parts of Christianity have tried to do, it will probably be the possibility of finding meaning that will be stressed.

Perhaps most dramatically for Christians in the last half century or so, Marxism has posed an understanding of the human situation that has had a profound impact on religion. The Marxist proposes that the principal problem in life consists in the repressive and exploitative character of social structures. The problem may be economic or it may rest on class bigotry or something else, but in each case it is the manner in which personal identity is controlled by the structures of the society that repress. The problem is not personal inadequacy. The Marxist understanding of the human dilemma has always affected the church, although often more negatively than positively. Millions of people, finding that they must choose between the church and Marxism, have affirmed the Marxist understanding of the human condition. In moments of superfluous generosity, one might almost excuse the church for its insistence that the choice be made, not only because of the human cruelty that characterizes most revolutions but particularly because the traditional Christian faith rests on quite another understanding of man. The sources of Christian faith do not support a Marxist interpretation of the world. Jesus was not a proto-Marxist. Jesus, who more than any other defines Christian existence, belongs clearly in the ethical tradition of Semitic origin in which interpersonal relationship is more important than social structure. As a matter of fact, social structure is of almost no concern at all to him.

Not even Jesus is absolute for the Christian. Not only because Jesus was plainly and simply wrong about the way history goes—the world did not come and is not coming to an astonishing end, at least not for supernatural reasons—but particularly because, for those of us in the twentieth century, Jesus has nothing to contribute regarding the social construction of human life, he cannot be absolute for us. Even having said that, it still is the case for many of us that Jesus occupies an incomparably important place in our understanding of who we are, of what life is about and might be, and of the way human existence might be redeemed. But he is not exhaustive. Jesus is not absolute. He cannot just be slipped into the place where God was. Still, beyond all others, he defines our hopes, our possibilities, our lives. The human community that we call church is shaped in response to his life and death. The Christian will sing his praises, rehearse his history, remember him with words and wine and bread, and perhaps even live and die for that dream, but the Christian also knows that someday Jesus will not occupy that position. The Jew who became a Christian still remembers Moses, but not as before. And the church has always known that, too. "Watch!" Christians have told each other. "The next time will be the greatest time of all, when everything will be made new."

That is the relative truth about Jesus.

The problem is how to know that everything is relative and at the same time satisfy those deep human needs for something to be committed to. We need a kind of stability, the kind of stability one might learn while running the deck of a rolling ship.

When Ivan in *The Brothers Karamazov* says, "If God does not exist, everything is permissable," he is *not* saying, "If my superego, in projected form, can be abolished, I can do anything with a good conscience." He *is* saying, "If there is *only* my conscience, then there is no ultimate validity for my will."[53]

It is not so much the prospect of anarchy that presses upon

us as it is vertigo. What kind of life commitments are available to us? What is their status and their validity? How does one choose between them? T. Patrick Burke says:

It makes a vast difference whether human life has a purpose, a goal, built into it, whether it already exists toward an ultimate realization, or whether in itself it is purposeless. In the first case life has "meaning" of itself; in the second case it is we who must give "meaning" to it by setting up our own goals.[54]

"What is the largest problem we face as human beings?" I asked a student.

"It is," she said, "that we spend our whole lives looking everywhere for some meaning in life, for some purpose to life, and there just isn't any to be found." I think she did not mean that the world is devoid of meanings, but that there is no evident validation for such meanings and purposes as we choose. "In the absence of a God, 'unsponsored' like the rest of their generation . . ."[55] as Sears and Lord described the writers whose works they examined, we get nervous and uncomfortable without something unquestionable to tie things to.

There is no evidence that the universe was planned, or that it is going anywhere in particular. "Chance *alone* is at the source of every innovation, of all creation in the biosphere," Jacques Monod says. "Pure chance, absolutely free but blind, at the very root of the stupendous edifice of evolution: this central concept of modern biology is no longer one among other possible or even conceivable hypotheses."[56] Where, then, did the notion ever come from that things had an aim or a purpose? Monod thinks we human beings read ourselves into the world around us. Plants grow, seek sunlight, and die, he says. Animals stalk their prey, fight, feed and protect their young, and breed. It seemed to our ancestors that everything had a purpose. And there were even more mysterious objects —rocks, rivers, mountains, thunderstorm, stars, and rain— and they too, if they existed must also surely have a purpose. They were invested, in the minds of our grandfathers, with souls, too. "In the river's depths, on the mountaintop, more subtle spirits pursue vaster and more impenetrable designs than the transparent ones animating man and beasts."[57] Everywhere there were forces at work, sometimes benign, sometimes hostile, but never totally alien. We knew what it meant to propose, to purpose, to aim, and we projected the forms of our own consciousness onto every other thing.

Evolution does not even aim for a consciousness such as ours, for evolution tries everything, although once mind and consciousness are there, nothing can be the same again. Mind is organization. It is transcendence. It intends and proposes. So far as we know purpose is born in the human mind, but once it is born there it permeates everything man touches. Kurt Vonnegut has a story about that:

In the beginning, God created the earth, and he looked upon it in His cosmic loneliness.

And God said, "Let us make living creatures out of mud, so the mud can see what We have done."

And God created every living creature that now moveth, and one was man. Mud as man alone could speak. God leaned close as mud as man sat up, looked around, and spoke. Man blinked. "What is the *purpose* of all this?" he asked politely.

"Everything must have a purpose?" asked God.

"Certainly," said man.

"Then I leave it to you to think of one for all this," said God. And He went away.[58]

Nicos Kazantzakis says, "The earth rises up in your brain; it sees for the first time its body whole and entire." In our brain, the earth remembers, ponders its passions, blooms, dominates time. "It is not my heart that beats and leaps in my blood, it is the whole earth. Turning back it relives its terrible ascent through chaos." The mind milks the universe.[59] A little bit of meaning is born like a thin blade of grass, trembling, in the human mind: "it milks the universe."

It seems to be the case not only that the human mind is capable of investing meaning and of constructing purposes but that the human mind must impose some kind of order and meaning on things. Not to do so is to risk inner disintegration and utter chaos. It may only be because the structures of the human mind itself drive toward intelligibility, but mind will seek meaning in the world of chance. Since meaning is not inherently there, mind constructs meaning. Perhaps that is only an instinctive drive for mental survival: it does not matter; it will, perhaps even must, be done.

"Structuring"—that is, providing abstract models which bear some coherent relation to the external world—continues to be the basic activity of the human mind whether in science, art, primitive thought, human play. . . . The implications . . . are staggering: most of what we mean by "reality" has been put together by our "symbol systems." Survivors of extreme experiences—the atomic holocaust, the concentration camps—bear witness to the irreducible necessity of structuring in human life.[60]

Bruno Bettelheim says that in prison camps in World War II it was the *senseless* tasks that were profoundly destructive. By destroying one's ability to act on one's own and to be able to predict the outcome of one's actions, the feeling that actions had any purpose was also destroyed, and life withered. Men became walking corpses. Only so long as a prisoner fought for survival, for self-assertion over against what seemed to be a senseless environment, was there a chance for life.[61]

In August 1967 Richard Rubenstein visited a mosque in Hebron that purports to contain the tombs of Abraham, Isaac, Jacob, Sarah, Rebeccah, and Leah. A group of Jews were there, and one chanted, "Praise be Thou, O Lord our God, God of Abraham, God of Isaac, and God of Jacob. . . ." "I felt," Rubenstein wrote, "that I had returned to my Father's house." More, he said that he grasped with clarity for the first time the knowledge that every religion is more than a community of common faith. Religion is an extension of home and the family. "All religious communities are kinship groups to some extent."[62] And then, speaking of what it means to be a nomadic people without holy places, Rubenstein wrote:

Archimedes believed that if he could find a fixed and unmovable point, he could move the entire world. Every man needs a fixed point of reference. The rapidity of our cultural and technological thrust precludes our finding any such points in our religious inheritance. Like the nomads of the desert, we shall flourish only if we discover resources for survival *within ourselves*. If we find any Archimedean point, it will be within. The security of home is only a memory. All we have left is the uncertain capacity to assume responsibility and direction over our own destinies. We cannot go home again.[63]

"Everything must have a purpose?" asked God.
"Certainly," said man.
"Then I leave it to you to think of one for all this," said God.

There may not be any purpose in the stars or in the atom, but apparently there must be purpose in man. There is purpose only in man. The universe has no intention, no goal. It is just there. Man intends. And when he does not intend, when he has no purpose, he is not man, either. There *is* meaning and purpose, then. We have it. It is as real as atoms and stars, and it is the way we organize the whirl around us. But there are no external ends to which we conform. That is unsettling. It is uncomfortable, and even maddening, but lamenting it doesn't change the way it is. The effect of knowing that purpose and meaning is something human ought not to be discouraging. The effect ought to be to realize that what man intends, what meanings he constructs, are incomparably important, precisely because there are none other. Man, as I will suggest later, has become an agent for the future.

"A religion presents us with a vision of life."[64]

Our view of the world and of ourselves has changed from something absolute to something relative, from something immobile to something moving. We are beginning to see how things turn, and become, and never go back. Teilhard de Chardin says that it

dates from the day when one man, flying in the face of appearance, perceived that the forces of nature are no more unalterably fixed in their orbits than the stars themselves, but that their serene arrangement around us depicts the flow of a tremendous tide— the day on which the first voice rang out, . . . "We are moving! We are going forward!"[65]

152

We are moving, going somewhere, and God cannot be the last immobile thing. It is a very difficult business to leave Egypt and become an exile people with no permanent place, a wandering people. After all these years of building houses, of making permanent places and putting our initials on stones, we find ourselves living in tents. We wrote perfect constitutions and held certain truths to be self-evident, and they are neither perfect nor self-evident. We even thought we had captured God and pinned him down with definitions and attributes. But there are no more permanent places, no more permanent ideas, no more permanent pictures of God.

"The denial of absolute truth is not an absolute denial of truth."[66]

CHAPTER 7

The Effect
of the Moon*

The exploration of space, particularly the manned exploration of space, has provoked a crisis in man's understanding of himself in relation to the world. Five times already, men from earth have sent fragile expeditions to go to and fro on the moon and walk up and down on it.

Five times the astronauts have brought back a suitcase full of rocks, and once they even left a microfilm of part of the Bible on the moon, along with a golf ball. Prayers from space have become part of the return liturgy. It is a curious business.

At first the exploration of space was great fun. President Kennedy said we could do it before 1970, and we did. By 1970, though, Americans were beginning to doubt it was worth all the money. After the third or fourth suitcase full of rocks, not even the prayers for peace from outer space were terribly convincing. The problem was that in the meantime "allied forces" had "defensively incurred" into two more Asian countries, poverty and the cities had gotten worse, and tunafish were eating the mercury we had dumped into the ocean. The air stank.

* Reprinted from *Dialog,* Spring 1972. Used by permission.

The very fact of tentative human capacity to *escape* from the earth—for however fleeting a time—has made us wonder about the ways in which we *belong* to the earth. The place of man in the world—his responsibility for it, his astonishing capacity to affect it, his identification with it—all these have impressed themselves into a dim new human self-understanding.

Our theological categories are at stake. The major terms of Christian discourse—sin, forgiveness, grace, love—have stressed the relationships of men to each other or of men to God. The world has for the most part been regarded as the arena in which the important activities of men took place. The world as *world*, and man's relationship to the world, have not occupied primary theological attention.

The task presented to theologians by this fresh attention to man and his place in the world is *not* to produce a theology for space (a kind of God for cosmic gaps) or a theology for ecology (a God for green growing things). The immediate job is much more that of articulating what this new relationship of man and world means for human self-understanding.

William Kuhns uses the word interface to describe man's relationship with someone or something else. Kuhns says:

What is at stake, finally, is the articulation of a badly needed Christian anthropology, which defines the whole man not in spite of the tendencies of the contemporary environment, but largely in terms of them.[1]

Man's contemporary environment is cosmic. The world isn't just there any longer; it is there at the mercy of man, the clumsy mercy of man, sometimes the perverse mercy of man. That is why one cannot any longer choose whether to direct attention to isolated man rather than to the whole world of nature in which man is embedded. Man and the whole world of nature come together, belong together, will survive or perish together. The ultimate symbol of man's relationship to the natural world used to be the bomb, which might destroy us all. Perhaps today our own garbage is a larger threat.

While the immediate attention of this chapter is focused on anthropology, my longer intention is to suggest the importance of a changing image of man for other theological issues, particularly the way in which our image of ourselves in the world has effect on the way we talk about God, and Jesus' relationship to God; and Jesus, as every Christian knows, is definitive for the community called the church. It is my intention to look at the shape of Christology in order to specify the human self-understandings inherent in Christological formulations. Precisely as is the case for the doctrine of God, the way we see ourselves, our problems and our possibilities, provides the basic shape of doctrines that grow out of that self-knowledge. It ought not to be an astonishment that our definitions of both Christology and of our language about God reflect our understanding of who we are, and who we think we are is not who we once thought we were.

In the patristic period, the formulations of Christology regularly turned on the question of the nature of man. If man is body and soul, and Christ is man, how then can one account for the wholeness of both his humanity and divinity without supposing him to be either more or less than man?

Already in the early fathers of the church the distinction between what has traditionally become "Eastern" and "Western" Christendom was evident, and at the heart of it were different apprehensions of the human situation. In the West, Christology was very soon effectively reduced to a question of how to speak of Christ in light of man as a moral offender against the holiness of God. Other understandings of Christ were not necessarily denied, or even lost, but the burning questions of man were moral.

The West has a characteristic "sin-and-forgiveness" Christology in which redemption is very much a matter of atonement. That is in evident contrast to an apprehension of the incarnation as the introduction of immortality into this mortal state, for instance, which is much more "Eastern" in its emphasis. The question of man has always been at the center of Christological discussion, although that has not always been recognized. That is particularly important to remember at a time, such as our own, when man's self-understanding is in question and in transition.

"If we rightly understand ourselves," Karl Barth said in *The Epistle to the Romans*, "our problems are the problems of

Paul; and if we be enlightened by the brightness of his answers, those answers must be ours."[2]

To the contrary, if we rightly understand ourselves, we must see that Paul's questions are *not* our questions; not so simply. There are indeed continuities in the human experience, and they may be long and powerful, but there is also change. "Here below to love is to change," Cardinal Newman said, "and to be perfect is to have changed often."[3] We simply do not understand ourselves, our problems and our potential, exactly the way Paul did. We put our questions otherwise, even our God questions, because we are in a different time and space—a different history. Paul is part of our history but not all of it, and he cannot forever say our questions and answers for us. We must finally ask what Jesus Christ can mean for such men as we know ourselves to be. That may indeed put us into conversation with Paul, but a conversation is not an echo.

We are in a new situation. Such a Christology as must be constructed for ourselves must grow out of our time and place. If one may borrow a term from Irenaeus,[4] we cannot simply "recapitulate" the past.

What follows here is not an attempt to articulate either a complete anthropology or Christology. It is an attempt to name some of the ways in which we are coming to understand our own humanity, in order to suggest the shape of the space Christology today must fill. These are, I think, some of the characteristics of man as we are beginning to realize ourselves.

THE ENERGY OF MAN

We are beginning to understand the energy of man. James Sellers, in an article titled "The Almost-Chosen People,"[5] proposed a distinction between the anthropologies inherent in much of the theology we have inherited and that of a theology more suitable to our own time.

The theological recovery of our own century, Sellers said, is largely characterized by a sixteenth-century way of organizing theology, namely, around a point of departure summed up as justification by faith alone. There is an assumed human helplessness inherent in that basic insight that is not helpful in the twentieth century. The sixteenth-century view of justification is tied, Sellers said, to an anthropology unable to account for the exploding initiative of secular man. "My problem, then," he said, "is not first with an obsolete doctrine of God, as with some of the 'God-is-dead' theologians, but rather with an obsolete doctrine of man."[6]

Sellers proposed several objections to the assumptions and effects of the doctrine of salvation by faith alone. Basic to them is the now untenable view of human capacity it assumes. Intended to guard against human pride and to assert the sufficiency of God, faith became a means of rescue for impotent men. The tendency was to stress passivity as a posture more amenable to God's purposes than initiative and activity. Even though both Luther and Calvin understood faith to consist *both* of a receptivity to that which is offered in divine grace *and* a state of grateful and active response empowered by that grace, nevertheless, natural or secular man was left in principle as impotent, strengthless, and passive. Sellers argues further:

It may be, indeed, that the chief problem of contemporary theology is not that God is dead, but that man is alive. It may be that even today we have not come resolutely to grips with the doctrine of man: his natural, unredeemed, secular initiative as a sign of his origin in the divine creation.[7]

Sellers' argument is that the assertion of human passivity is not inherently a better way of accounting for the activity of God in salvation than is human activity. We are living in what Edward T. Hall calls an "ageric" culture (from Latin *agere,* to act), Sellers said. One of the results of contrasting the vigor of God with the weakness of man is to suggest the meaninglessness of the world. And that is precisely contrary to the experience of a man who knows that life is not meaningless at all but highly productive of satisfying meanings. The theological seesaw we have accepted, in which the elevation of God requires a contrasting downgrading of man, or in which the elevation of man requires the death of God, proffers a false choice. Man's problem is not that he is naturally weak but that he is too strong, too able, and too likely to find too much meaning in the immensely tempting, small, limited, and confining areas of life. "Saving grace is not 'strength' of some kind, for we already have plenty of that; grace is direction, a sense of time and terrain, a comprehension of values on the plane of creation, and the gift of moving into the presence of God and the others."[8]

It is quite evident, if Sellers is right, that the manner in which one will describe the saving activity of Jesus Christ will be sharply affected by such an ageric man as he understands us to be. "Human beings," he said, "are, in general, God's 'almost chosen people,' capable of advancing into new, restored humanity, which is incipiently and even provisionally good—but not good enough."[9] Man's end will be to find wholeness of humanity in history, not somewhere else, for time and space are meaningful, and Christ must then be an instance of that new humanity, furnishing a criterion of human initiative and action that *really* represents God at work.[10]

Whether Christ is more or less than that, one must agree with Sellers that any theology that presupposes the helplessness of man will run counter to evident human experience. One might still propose that the displayed energy of man is precisely of the essence of man's sin, but even then the discourse must assume (for good or ill) that man presupposes not weakness but vitality. In the twentieth century, one might only by might and main make converts to the notion of human impotence, and that is a self-contradictory exercise. Carl Sandburg expressed his own wonder at the energy of man this way:

> When one tall skyscraper is torn down
> To make room for a taller one to go up
> Who takes down and puts up
>   those skyscrapers?
> Man—the little two-legged
>   joker . . . MAN.[11]

No Christology can seriously be considered in our time in history that rests, at bottom, on the helplessness of man. Contemporary theology must begin with the capability of man, sometimes the perverted capability, but capability nonetheless.

THE MALLEABILITY OF MAN

New in human experience is a recognition of the malleability of man.[12] Men wonder today what it means for man to have a nature, or more, whether it makes any sense to say that man has a nature. Artemus Ward used to say that everybody has as much human nature as everybody else, if not more.[13]

Not only Christology but Christian theology in general has assumed a kind of Aristotelian hierarchy of things, with man located somewhere above potatoes and bullfrogs and somewhat below more angelic beings. To speak of man in that hierarchical way is to suppose a kind of eternal form or substance for man in which his possibilities are forever predetermined, spoiled only by the flaw that the fall into sin introduces into those eternal potentialities. That way of understanding human existence is not very biblical. The language of substance and nature is strange to scripture. The language of action is not.

Probably the most beautiful and perhaps also the most profound understanding of man as an unfinished creature is that of Teilhard de Chardin. His whole book *The Phenomenon of Man*[14] is an orchestration of the process by which the earth has curved in upon itself, first to organize itself into something that lives and finally into life that not only is conscious but that is self-conscious: man.

Man came silently into the world, Teilhard said, sprawling everywhere with stone instruments in his hand. Man, for Teilhard, is not simply the best that the animal kingdom could produce. As silently as he came, man was the product of a general groping of the world, the descendent of the total effort of life. This groping of the world toward ever more complex forms of expression is evolution, and evolution, he said, "is a general condition to which all theories, all hypotheses, all systems must bow and which they must satisfy henceforward if they are to be thinkable and true. Evolution is a light illuminating all facts, a curve that all lines must follow."[15] And that which characterizes modern man, he continued, is the incapability of seeing anything otherwise, even himself. Man could not see evolution all around him and not feel carried along by it himself. Teilhard said, "The consciousness of each of us is evolution looking at itself and reflecting."[16]

Theodosius Dobzhansky makes the same point, suggesting that the most significant point in Darwin's teachings is often ignored, to wit, "Man has not only evolved, he is evolving."[17] Man, and man alone, knows he is evolving, Dobzhansky says, and he knows that when he changes the world he changes himself.

As it dawns upon man that there is neither eternal form nor substance defining him, and as he realizes that what he is today is just the most recent shape of things that have been, man cannot but wonder what he shall tomorrow be. But best (or worst) yet, what man shall be tomorrow is what man shall make of himself. Evolution is no more an unconscious groping toward organization, toward life, or even toward consciousness. Evolution has come to an awareness of itself in man. Coupled with a recognition of man's own astounding wit and energy, evolution has become capable of maneuvering its own course. It has not yet been decided what man shall be, and it shall not be decided until man knows what he wants to be and how.

The decision is not optional. Some decisions about man's future have already been made. The enormous problems that the human race faces with overpopulation are in large measure due to man's effective, though limited, control of death. The use of medicine and an understanding of disease have made it possible for people who might never have survived without help to live into adulthood and long life. No one is proposing that such negative eugenic controls be abandoned. The problem is felt most keenly with the possibility for positive eugenic manipulation. That raises all kinds of questions about which more must be said shortly.

When there is no abiding answer to the question of what a human being is, and when the real question becomes what man intends to *become,* other questions about the nature and salvation of man are suddenly put into a whole new context and given new form. Then one cannot seriously talk about salvation as if it were a recovery of what man once was. Christ is then no restoration but a clarification, a possibility, and a promise of what one might become.

A NEW APPRECIATION OF MAN IN NATURE

We have further begun to realize our complete involvement with the world of nature. Loren Eiseley, who does not know how to write pedestrian prose, whose books are an ecstasy of unmetered poetry, tells in *The Immense Journey* of the time he saw chemicals fly. With a knapsack full of the petrified bones of creatures no more seen, he stood at sunset on a cold autumn day in a wasted place and thought about the ground. Under his feet lay fifty million years of residue of earlier times, stones now sand, peppered with the carbon remains of a once green place, and overhead a flight of birds made their way south.

The chemicals of all that vanished age lay about me in the ground. Around me still lay the shearing molars of dead titanotheres, the delicate sabers of soft-stepping cats, the hollow sockets that had held the eyes of many a strange, outmoded beast. Those eyes had looked out upon a world as real as ours; dark, savage brains had roamed and roared their challenges into the steaming night. Now they were still here, or, put it as you will, the chemicals that made them were here about me in the ground. . . . I lifted up a fistful of that ground. I held it while that flight of southbound warblers hurtled over me into the oncoming dark. There went phosphorus, there went iron, there went carbon, there beat the calcium in those hurrying wings.

"What did you see?" his drowsy friend asked him at camp.

"I think a miracle."[18]

There are men who see in the world a kind of wholeness of things, who speak as if the world, here and there, had so organized itself that sometimes it lived and moved. We *are* the development of the earth. We *are* moving, as are the stars and stones. Mankind, he thought, was divided into two irrevocably divided camps—"one looking towards the horizon and proclaiming with all its new-found faith, 'We are moving,' and the other, without shifting its position, obstinately maintaining, 'Nothing changes. We are not moving at all.' "[19]

For some men the world is an immobile place, always the same, always in place. For those men God is the unmoved mover, perfect, like cut glass.

It has taken the simple fact of our identification with the world a long time to sift down into the recesses of our consciousness. It is the earth, with a movement and a direction so obscure we are not sure it is purposeful, that has given birth to life and to man.

Once men could imagine that life was an intrusion into the world and man a transient. Now we know that man is as natural here as the hardest stone and the passing breeze.

The Cartesian dualism that has structured so much of Christian thinking about salvation, a dualism that tended inevitably to posit an eternal distinction and separate values for body and mind, cannot be retained. Soul salvation, escape-hatch Christology, is completely contrary to the way we know we are.

We know we are matter called to life, to become incarnate minds. Pieter de Jong says if we interpret God's breathing the breath of life into man in a dualistic manner, as told in Genesis 2:7, then man receives some kind of divine spark from God. But, he argues, if we are faithful to Hebrew thought, we must take that passage to mean that God's creative power calls man to life. "The breath of God gives life to man and beast . . . and to the entire creation. . . . If God withholds his breath, man dies. . . . The only hope for immortality would be if God continued to address man beyond death."[20]

Men do not come in parts, some parts potentially eternal and some temporary. Saved or damned, man is one. We are of, and not just in, the world. Nature, then, whether we speak of our own physical nature or of the physical world beyond us, is not something to be fought and overcome, as if it were an outside enemy.

André Malraux, speaking of an underlying cause of the rebellion of students, denied that it was simply a conflict of generations. The dilemma of the young, he said, is but one aspect of the most basic problem of our generation, which is built around machines and neglects man. A civilization of machines can teach man everything except how to be a man.

In all of the great civilizations of the past, there was a harmony between man and the universe. . . . Even civilizations which were not religious, like Greece, had it. Bon. Now we, for the first time, we have a knowledge of matter and a knowledge of the universe which suppresses man. He has no importance. The theory of Einstein does not involve man except through his thinking. But the universe . . . our concept of it . . . is independent from man. . . . It is extremely difficult to envisage a civilization which accepts a complete rupture between man and the universe. . . . And so there is this extraordinary malaise, especially among the young.[21]

MAN OUT OF HARMONY

There are two sides to this lack of harmony between man and the universe. The first, the delusion that what constitutes "real man" is finally not physical, has already been suggested. The second side is almost more serious—that is, to regard the world as ultimately of lesser worth and, since of lesser worth, an expendable resource.

History will certainly demonstrate that it was during the last half of the twentieth century that men suddenly realized how tightly their own survival was bound up with the survival of the whole earth. The exploration of space—particularly the landing of men on the moon—has caused us to realize what a rare and fragile thing life is and what a hostile and unforgiving thing space is. There is bitter irony in the recognition that, just when we are able to lift ourselves off the earth, this earth is still the only environment in which we can survive.

At the same time, human survival on earth is very much in question. Human progress has been fueled by the unreflective consumption and alteration of the resources of the earth. Natural fuels are being exhausted. Rivers are filthy. (The Ohio River is so polluted with oil waste that it will burn.) Nearly every major city realizes the air it needs is just short of being unbreathable. Whether wildlife can survive with man is questionable. Politicians are beginning to speak of "ecology" and "environment" and "pollution," a sure sign that the problem of man's relationship to the rest of the physical world is becoming desperate.

A recent conference in Alaska proposed that the despoiling of the world around us is rooted in a Judeo-Christian ethic that views the world as put here for the benefit and enjoyment of man—an extension, so to speak, of the Garden of Eden. Oriental philosophies, it was argued in contrast, see man as a part of nature, called upon to live in harmony with it.[22]

Victor Ferkiss, in his excellent book *Technological Man: The Myth and the Reality,* argues the same case. Rivers of ink, he says, have been expended on the alleged role of Puritanism in the rise of capitalism and the whole question of the "Protestant Ethic." Not merely Puritanism or Protestantism but Western Christianity itself is at the root of the new manipulative, domineering attitude toward the world that has been the fundamental intellectual precondition of the rise of industrialism. Further, Ferkiss charges that implicit in Christianity was a basically hostile attitude toward nature, expressing itself "in the idea that creation was a gift of God to man, to be used by him. Use meant exploitation, and eventually manipulation and even destruction."[23]

It is precisely at this point that Western Christology does indeed need such a corrective as Eastern Christology can provide. Without arguing whether Eastern churches have managed in the course of history to avoid regarding the world as essentially alien, a stockpile of goods to be consumed, wasted, or fought, there are clear reminders in Eastern tradition, as can be noted in the theology of Irenaeus, for instance, that man is so inherently involved with the nature and destiny of the world that he cannot simply spend it as extra coin. Creation is a totality. It is unethical and dangerous to destroy one part of it for another, whether the part destroyed be mute or whether the beneficiary be man. It is becoming evident to us that when nature is plundered man impoverishes himself. The world is not a barbarian to be tamed, an enemy to be fought. It ought, rather, to be appreciated, saved, cooperated with, and granted such a measure of respect as the ancestor of us all deserves.

"The whole problem is one of human ecology," said George Schaller, who learned something about the nature of man by following gorillas about.

Man is conquering the diseases that once kept his population in check, and he is spreading his sway, exterminating other animals and exhausting the soil. With the same mentality that once enabled him to vanquish the lion and the bear, he is trying to subdue nature, sacrificing the eternal for the expedient. The destruction of the earth lies at his whim and cunning, yet he does not realize, does not feel, that he is not separate from but one with plants and animals, rock and water. He is as dependent on them as the protozoan, the tsetse, and the gorilla. By setting himself apart from the ecological community man has become a tyrant of the earth, but a tyrant who surely will fall if he succeeds in winning the struggle for existence.[24]

"Man," Julian Huxley said, "can no longer regard himself so complacently as the lord of creation or the conqueror of nature. He must be a partner with nature, a responsible partner."[25] Ferkiss, again, says our astronauts are a symbol of the new involvement of men with their physical environment, but perhaps only the most obvious and colorful representatives of what man has become.[26]

That is man, so inextricably bound up with the universe that it is hopeless to talk of his nature and destiny if one does not at once talk about him with his world.

What might salvation mean for such a man? Surely not to rescue him from what he is, the one known instance in which the universe has organized itself into a thinking, responsible being. If Christians ever again pretend that the good life, the saved life, is to be gained by turning away from the natural physical world or from one's own physical world or from one's own physical nature, the results will probably be disastrous. Not by denying but by valuing the place of man in nature will either man or nature survive. Man is not otherworldly. He isn't a spirit. He *has* spirit.

MAN AS AGENT FOR THE FUTURE

The promise and the problem of man is experienced most acutely when it is realized that men have become what Huxley again called agents for the future.[27]

Whether there was purpose and intentionality in the universe before the emergence of man is a curious and hopeless question. But now there are men, and now there is intention. There was always evolution. Teilhard, for instance, believed that he saw an inherent logic in the development of evolution from simple physical complexity, through such sentient complexity as produces mind, to human consciousness and perhaps beyond to something called Omega. What is certain is that, with man, evolution is at a state in which its possibilities are open to deliberate manipulation by man.

Man, alone among all organisms, knows that he evolves and he alone is capable of directing his own evolution. For him evolution is no longer something that happens to the organism regardless, but something in which the organism may and must take an active hand.[28]

Few men have been more enthusiastic about aggressive human involvement in the course that evolution shall take than Hermann J. Muller. Already in 1935 he had a vision of nearly unlimited human development. He believed there would be three main stages in the history of life. Natural selection governed a long preparatory phase, in which life was gradually ground into human shape. A second and short transitional stage followed (our own stage), in which life reaches out at the immediate environment,

shaking, shaping, and grinding it to suit the form, the requirements, the wishes, and the whims of man. And in the long third phase it will reach down into the secret places of the great universe of its own nature and, by the aid of its evergrowing intelligence and cooperation, shape itself into an increasingly sublime creation—a being beside which the mythical divinities of the past will seem more and more ridiculous, and which, setting its own marvelous inner powers against the brute Goliath of the suns and planets, challenges them to contest.[29]

The dream behind all human research, Teilhard said, is fundamentally that of mastering the process of change itself "by grasping the very mainspring of evolution, seizing the tiller of the world."[30] Even before he realized he had the tiller in his hand, man had begun to affect the course of his own evolution. He did it with medicine. When, for instance, the application of insulin makes it possible for uncounted

numbers of people to survive and reproduce who might otherwise have died, the next generation of human beings is already altered.[31] Should, for instance, mentally inferior or de-
ranged persons be allowed to reproduce?

To answer that question one must decide to what extent
intelligence or mental illness is inherited and to what degree
a society has a right to make such determinations for an
individual. As long as medical science was more a matter of
good intention than realization, it made sense to say that it
was always more virtuous to save a life. But today, as
Edmund Leach pointed out, doctors, provided with adequate
resources, can preserve alive all manner of deformed infants
and senile invalids who would, in the natural course of
events, have long since died. "At some point the burden will
become intolerable, and saving life will become morally
evil."[32] The point has already been reached, and decisions
are already being made to allow some people to live and
others to die, and very few people enjoy making the choices.
There already is genetic control of a negative sort, and man
is planning his own future.

As certain as the dawn, the day must soon come when
men, perhaps by chemical genetic manipulation, will be able
to do something about the kind of people we shall be. Perhaps someone will decide that people should not be so hostile,
and that hostility, however it is caused, should be suppressed.
Maybe that will lower the crime rate in Chicago and Buenos
Aires and make wars much less likely. It might at the same
time produce such a race of shy sheep that even normal
aggressiveness and initiative are destroyed. As James Sellers
pointed out, man is not helpless but strong. He is an agent
for the future with only the slightest notions about which
way to go.

A NEW SENSE OF BEING LOST

Our involvement with the world of nature and our inescapable
roles as agents for the future confront us with a new apprehension of evil. We are overcome with a malady of aimlessness, the lack of a sense of direction.

Judged by any reasonable criteria, Theodosius Dobzhansky
said,

man represents the highest, most progressive, and most successful product of organic evolution. . . . Most remarkable of all, he is now in the process of acquiring knowledge which may permit him, if he so chooses, to control his own evolution. He may yet become "business manager for the cosmic process of evolution," a role which Julian Huxley has ascribed to him, perhaps prematurely.[33]

The evidence is that once man puts his plans into effect, their realization is worse than their intention. The planned society, John Greene says, looks less inviting in its grim reality than it did when still a dream.[34]

"He who fights the future," Sören Kirkegaard said, "has a dangerous enemy. The future is not, it borrows its strength from the man himself, and when it has tricked him out of this, then it appears outside of him as the enemy he must meet."[35] It may be that the salvation of man has been his own stupidity, his own incapacity to implement such plans as he has made for his own future and that of the world. Too often, like DDT in our food, our best intentions descend upon our heads to demonstrate how great an evil is a little knowledge and a lot of nerve.

The church today does not know what it ought to be or ought to do. Once Americans knew what their destiny was: to make the world safe for democracy, or perhaps to nurture rugged individualism. No one really knows what to do any longer about the racial turmoil in America or Africa. No one knows how to eliminate war. Everyone knows that if we do not eliminate war, we will probably eliminate life itself. It has not always been that way. Man's very inventiveness has not only made him his own worst enemy but also made him responsible in larger ways than ever before. The privilege of wandering through history is gone. Man must *intend*.

The aimlessness of man is based on his own confusion about what a man should be.

In the long run the fate of civilization depends not only on its political system, its economic structure, or its military might. Perhaps, indeed, all of these ultimately depend in turn upon the faith of the people, upon what we believe and feel about Man; about the possibilities of human nature.[36]

Assuming that man is indeed something like what we have been describing, what then? "Good enough," Clifford Grobstein says:

Now what can we do with man? He is a director and arranger of the environment at a new level. He not only manipulates sticks and strings, he even rearranges the lives of many of the other species within the biomass. He learns to do tricks with fundamental energy sources and has the power to alter the properties of the whole biosphere. On the one hand, he tinkers with molecular messages that underlie the entire fabric of life; on the other, he stands ready to step off the earth and lead a boarding party to other planets.*

Once men thought that such remarkable potential as they possessed would result in an Orwellian world in which every breath and every move would be controlled. It is quite likely, Ferkiss points out, that not tyranny but sheer chaos threatens us, "an intensification of the experience of those who have had difficulties over their income tax or been incorrectly billed for a credit purchase or a long-distance call."[37] Man isn't weak; he is powerful, and he must devise his own future. The problem is: which future? Which direction?

It does not make any sense to talk about Jesus Christ as if he were the ultimate in relief from moral guilt, or as if he were the absolute antidote to our temporality, when concern for guilt and death are not really the demons that keep men awake nights. If the human dilemma is much more the problem of what to become, of which direction to go, of what a man should be, Christological discourse must speak with such language.

Man carries his future in himself, and Christology must be eschatological in the sense that it recognizes that what shall be is not yet realized and that the future really is open. The classical human problems with which Christology has dealt—problems of morality and mortality—do not properly describe contemporary man.

That is not to say that sin and death are not both genuine

---

* From *The Strategy of Life* by Clifford Grobstein, p. 111. W. H. Freeman & Company. Copyright © 1965.

and present. They are. But they do not suggest what is particular to the present human situation. We are much more
like Charlie Gordon in David Roger's play *Flowers for
Algernon,* who, having been brought from retardation to
genius and knowing that he was returning again to an almost
subhuman level of mental life, said, "I'm afraid, not of life
or death or nothingness, but of wasting it, as if I had never
been."[38] Carl Braaten insists that death is as large a problem
for people as always: "Of all the silly things that are said,
surely the silliest is that 'modern man is no longer afraid of
death.' "[39] Perhaps Carl Braaten is right. One might be able
to demonstrate, even statistically, that most people are afraid
to die. We could surely *hope* that most human beings are
reluctant to die; life ought to be at least that enjoyable. But
we are not counting heads here, for a majority vote and rule:
fifty million Frenchmen *can* be wrong. The question is much
more whether, for those who do not define their lives by sin
and death, a theology committed to that discourse can hold
promise and power enough to shape life. I think not.

Neither can we recapture again the power that neo-
orthodoxy had during and after World War II. That power
depended upon a sense of meaninglessness or helplessness
that simply does not describe us well.

James Sellers is right about that: we don't feel weak; we
know we are strong. Contemporary anguish is much more a
question of what to do with human powers and possibilities.
Everything we discover we can do seems to have a destructive side to it. Nuclear energy and DDT and internal combus-
tion engines and supersonic airplanes and oil wells and
genetic engineering are nearly as threatening as they are
promising. The evident fact that human beings make a mess
of almost everything cannot be used as a reason for a return
to more comfortable days when we told our heavenly Father
about it and told each other that God would make it good
again. There is no effective escape in nostalgia; we have
there no abiding home. Everyone knows that technological
capabilities will not go away, no matter how badly they are
applied. It ought not to be surprising that much of contemporary theology has to do with future and hope and even
a finer world to come. For precisely the same reasons, reac-

tionary theologies look good to a lot of people. They are a reaffirmation of what once clearly was so—a simpler world. Surprising numbers of young people, whom one might suppose would be most ready to try new worlds, are proclaiming something remarkably like old-time religion. They have seen the problems and withdrawn from them. The problems will not disappear. The question is how to manage them. The future *is* both promising and threatening, and more than ever before in human history the future is a planned future. Planning is exhilarating only so long as the one who is planning knows in which direction to go. Conversely, to be responsible for human destiny without really knowing what men should be with each other, and become, is a terrible kind of lostness, a contemporary kind of lostness. The problem of not knowing what to do, and of having to do it nonetheless, may be a far better way to describe the dilemma of man than any amount of talk about moral degeneracy or inherent mortality.

That is why theology must have to do with the future, not in the sense of eschatological escape from this human world of responsibility but in the sense of that toward which we move—with a sense of direction.

What is new for us again (since this has happened before) is man's own apprehension of himself. Man does not see himself in relation to the world and to other men in quite the same way as before, and as a consequence, when he speaks of Jesus Christ, he speaks in not quite the same way as before.

Jesus stands there in history, a man of whom other men have said the most remarkable things. *What* men have said about Jesus varies nearly as much as the men who said it. There is not the slightest hope that someday, somewhere, someone will remember or discover or construct the one completely satisfying, ultimately valid Christology. There is a very good chance that we may do what men before us have done—that is, to come to terms with Jesus and to say, as it seems to us, what he is all about and what then we are all about.

Teilhard said man has his hand on the tiller of the world and he is going somewhere. Man is finally beginning to understand what it is to create and to destroy. Man has learned how to live in space before he has learned how to live with himself.

If Jesus is the revelation of God, then God must have to do with the possibilities for people to become people with each other, and for the world, which has learned in us to reflect and to intend, to move with care.

Perhaps we should say that redemption is a new possibility for man to realize his humanity.

CHAPTER 8

A Vision
of
Life

L et's play a word association game," the host at the party said. (The "party" was filmed by the Franciscan Communications Center—one of their television spot announcements.) "Money. Dentist. Clothes. Money." The words tumbled over each other. And then the host said, "God."

Complete silence. Nothing.

"God," he said again.

Paul van Buren has decided that it does mean something to talk about God, if it be properly understood.[1] It is a mistake, though, he maintains, to suppose language about God is straightforward language about a being who acts, loves, and judges as people do. (There seems to be a good amount of Ian Ramsey in van Buren's latest book, although Ramsey is never mentioned.) Van Buren says to speak of God is to walk along the borders of language. Not to realize that, to speak of a God who acts as a personal agent, is to court nonsense because "it is notoriously the case that neither this agent nor the effects of his agency can be distinguished. If God is an agent, then his agency seems to have no ascertainable effects upon the course of this world."[2] That is the dilemma of the theist who affirms certain acts as divine and who always has difficulty describing to others how those acts or events differ from other ordinary happenings. God's agency seems to other men to be inascertainable.

Some men claim to see God almost everywhere. For them the world pulses with the being and activity of God, and they are mystified and even sometimes offended that otherwise sensible and adequately intelligent people cannot see what they see. As an example, consider B. H. Liddell-Hart's words:

I will state very simply how I came to find evidence of God that was convincing to reason. It was that an unworldly current of goodness has been maintained, and proved insuppressible, in a world where evil flourishes and selfishness has obvious advantages. By human standards there is no sense in self-sacrifice and helping others at one's own expense. Yet that unselfish motive has been manifested in innumerable cases. Can it be explained save by the presence of a higher source of inspiration?[3]

Self-sacrifice and kindness *can* be explained without recourse to a higher source of inspiration, without God, but that would seem preposterous to people like Liddell-Hart. One might accuse him of having a very jaundiced view of the world, but that, too, is part of the way he "sees." For people like him, both the agent and his agency are everywhere evident. Even more striking was a recent letter from Beatrice Short Neall to the editor of *Time* magazine.

God is the keystone to an understanding of the universe and man. Take him out, and the structure falls into a heap of meaningless pieces. The universe becomes a chance arrangement of atoms. and man becomes an accident, a beast, or a machine.

But put the keystone back in, and the universe is seen as an orderly, fantastically complex system directed by infinite intelligence. Science and theology become parts of a unified field of knowledge, and human existence once again becomes meaningful.[4]

The understanding of God expressed in that letter is both

beautiful and a beautiful *example* of the way in which God has served as a perspective by which to hold all things together. God is a world view, an organizing principle, a *personal* organizing principle, by which to see the heap of pieces of which the world is comprised. Some people do see the world that way. But it is just as clearly true that other people do *not* see an infinite intelligence all around. They do see a chance arrangement of atoms, and man as an accident. But that is not regarded as a cause for alarm. It is still, for them too, "an orderly, fantastically complex system," but the lack of a divine person to direct everything is not necessarily to sink into meaninglessness. If man is a machine, he is a meaning-making machine. Meanings and purposes may not be indelibly printed on the night sky, but only seldom have human beings found themselves without what James Sellers called "a sense of time and terrain."

There is a great divide. The division is in how we see. Teilhard de Chardin described his own understanding of reality that way: "It is this cry, and this alone, which I wish to make here—the cry of one who thinks he sees."[5] We all look at the same world. Some see a person or something personal there, and some do not. God is the keystone for some, holding everything together. For others, the world and life invite meaning but do not provide it. Antony Flew's paraphrase of John Wisdom's parable may still be the best illustration of our situation:

Once upon a time two explorers came upon a clearing in the jungle. In the clearing were growing many flowers and many weeds. One explorer says, "Some gardener must tend this plot." The other disagrees. "There is no gardener." So they pitch their tents and set a watch. No gardener is ever seen. "But perhaps he is an invisible gardener." So they set up a barbed-wire fence. They electrify it. They patrol it with bloodhounds. (For they remember how H. G. Wells' *The Invisible Man* could be both smelt and touched though he could not be seen.) But no shrieks ever suggest that some intruder has received a shock. No movements of the wire ever betray an invisible climber. The bloodhounds never give cry. Yet still the Believer is not convinced. "But there is a gardener, invisible, intangible, insensible to electric shocks, a gardener who has no scent and makes no sound, a gardener who comes secretly to look after the garden which he loves." At last the Skeptic despairs. "But what remains of your original assertion? Just how does what you call an invisible, intangible, eternally elusive gardener differ from an imaginary gardener or even from no gardener at all?"[6]

"A fine brash hypothesis may thus be killed by inches." Flew says, "the death of a thousand qualifications."[7]

Flew called his explorers the Skeptic and the Believer. Perhaps in the mid-1950s, when Flew published that essay, that is how the division was made. We still divide ourselves into those who see a Gardener and those who do not, but today the names are wrong. They are, at least, not *necessarily* right. The issue now is not so much between those who say God (or Gardener) and those who do not, but what it *means* to say God. The question is whether it can mean anything significant to say God but not Gardener. If that is not possible, large numbers of human beings are either going to have to abandon their intention and inclination to affirm the significance of religion, since no one can by simple exercise of willpower shift back to an already abandoned world view, or else learn a kind of schizophrenic accommodation to two incongruous world views. I do not mean to suggest it is a kind of illness to regard God as a Gardener or Mechanic or Personal Friend. I do mean that it is nearly impossible to see the world as if it were being manipulated, however graciously, by someone—someone whose presence holds atoms and worlds and stars and people meaningfully together—and at the same time know in the context of most of our transactions with the world that destiny is not written in the stars, that everything does depend on the course we choose, however blindly we must choose it and accept its consequences. That is to have two minds about things. That is to see in incompatible ways, and that is possible. Men do pray for rain on Sunday morning and seed the clouds on Monday, although, as Thomas Huxley once said, "even parish clerks doubt the utility of prayers for rain, so long as the wind is in the east."[8] It is possible on Sunday morning to believe steadfastly that diseases can be cured by the casting out of demons, but it is best on Monday to take one's medicine. In fact, so long as God is conceived of as a superperson, one *must* live in two worlds and simply do the best one can to keep them separate, or invent ingenious explanations for the ways in which those world views collide. They are not compatible.

In her letter to *Time* magazine, Beatrice Short Neall mentioned the reason why it is so difficult to consider seeing everything from another perspective: everything falls apart. God has been the explanation for how everything is. By definition, to let go of God (in that sense) is to let go of coherence. If a personal God is how things hold together, then to deny that such a person exists is at the same time to abandon the only known reason for coherence. At least it must seem that way until one has found some other way to think of things. That, of course, is the threat inherent in giving up belief in a personal God. God is the explanation for everything. God is a world view. God is seen as the director of "an orderly, fantastically complex system." It is no small decision to shift to another way of seeing everything. For some it is impossible, even appearing to be madness. Or, as Ivan said, "If God does not exist, all things are permitted."

Nietzsche knew what was at stake; that was his particular genius. In *Thus Spake Zarathustra,* the disciples of Zarathustra asked him what was the moral of his story, and he responded, "The destroyer of mortality, the good and the just call me: my story is immoral."[9] Nietzsche did not consider himself immoral. The good and the just did, because Nietzsche destroyed the foundations of *their* morality. It was precisely morality that Nietzsche was about. But he wanted to establish morality on some basis other than God. If that were not done, Nietzsche agreed that "morality from henceforward—there is no doubt about it—goes *to pieces*: this is that great hundred-act play that is reserved for the next two centuries of Europe, the most terrible, the most mysterious, and perhaps also the most hopeful of all plays."[10]

Nietzsche thought the English had the most trouble recognizing what was at stake. The English, he thought, acted as if the loss of God, serious as that was, still left one with Christian morality, and that, for a duty-bound people, was a peculiar comfort. Nietzsche said that for Christians morality was something God gives: man cannot know what is good or bad for him. So then, if belief in God is wrenched away, the morality is torn away, too. "Nothing vital remains within our grasp. . . . When we renounce the Christian faith, we abandon all right to Christian morality."[11]

Werner Heisenberg recognized the same dilemma. He said:

In western culture, for instance, we may well reach the point in the not too distant future where the parables and images of the old religion will have lost their persuasive force even for the average person; when that happens, I am afraid that all the old ethics will collapse like a house of cards and that unimaginable horrors will be perpetrated.[12]

And it is so. The two-hundred-year-long drama is being played out. Who then shall define crime? Who shall decide what is good and what is evil? They were not *our* values. We belonged to *them*.[13] Had they been our values, our creations, we might simply have reexamined them and refashioned them. But they were a gift to us. So all things are permitted, at least until we establish an alternate basis for morality, and that, of course, is what Nietzsche intended to do, however adequately he was able. "Somebody else," Tillich said about Nietzsche's system, "must replace God as the bearer of the system of traditional values. This is man."[14]

There *must* be a replacement for the traditional notion of God. God, in that sense, has occupied far too large a space in human life simply to vacate. In 1959, Carl Jung wrote a letter to a pastor of the Swiss Reformed Church who had asked about the possibility of a religionless Christianity. Jung thought that people were "faith tired and exhausted from the strain of sustaining notions which are not clearly understood by them and thus do not seem worth believing."[15] To be "religionless," Jung said, is not to be without myth. One needs myth, whether the myth be God, a Savior, a philosophical idea, or an ethical principle. But, Jung said, the traditional mythical concepts of faith demand too much effort of a contemporary person to believe. In earlier centuries, when people knew less, that was not so. No sacrifice of the intellect was needed to affirm a miracle or to regard the account of the Savior (resurrection, etc.) as biography. But now, "the teaching of the Trinity, the divine nature of the Savior, the incarnation of the Holy Spirit, the miracles of Jesus and his resurrection no longer evoke belief, but doubt."[16] Myths, Jung argued, refer to something, probably to what is commonly called religious experience. Given those finally inexpressible experiences, mythical images and names make what is otherwise a solitary experience common property. Myths make religious community possible. Jung thought that myths needed to be interpreted, given new forms, not eliminated. The error was either to underrate those archetypal myths as "mere instincts" or to overrate them as "gods." In either case, the real danger would be to destroy them without putting something in their place. "The danger of a final destruction is grave considering that even theologians begin to dismantle the classical, mythical world of perception without replacing it with a new possibility of experience."[17] In the terms that I have been using here, it would be dangerous to pull out the conception of God as a personal being, whose existence gives meaning to everything, without rethinking the ways in which meaning—even similar meaning—can otherwise be affirmed. Or, in the terms of the *Time* letter, if God is the keystone to an understanding of the universe and man, to pull God out is to make a heap of the structure. World views are at stake.

In *Kirillov's Quest,* Dostoevski has Kirillov say: "Man has done nothing but invent God so as to go on living, and not kill himself; that's the whole of universal history up till now. I am the first one in the whole history of mankind who would not invent God. Let them know it once for all." Listening to Kirillov, Fyodor Stepanovich thought, "He won't shoot himself."[18]

Paul Tillich once remarked that, when he was young, boys of seventeen or so read Nietzsche and then committed suicide. His own life was spared, Tillich said, because he did not read Nietzsche until he was somewhat older.

If Nietzsche and Jung and Tillich and Dostoevski and the people who write letters to *Time* magazine are correct, some of the peculiar language of the God-is-dead theologians begins to make some sense. Susan Taubes writes:

He who, seeking God, does not find him in the world, he who suffers the utter silence and nothingness of God, still lives in a religious universe: a universe whose essential meaning is God, though that meaning be torn in contradiction and the most agonizing paradoxes. He lives in a universe that is absurd, but whose absurdity is significant, and its significance is God. God, however negatively conceived, explains the world, explains the nothingness of God in the world.[19]

In any straightforward view, that is nearly indistinguishable from nonsense. God is dead, but the presence of his nothingness gives meaning to the world! (Should there be a fine for people who insist, in the best German manner, of speaking of nothingness as if it were somethingness?) What lies beneath statements of that kind, I think, is the human necessity to see sense in things. Chaos must be denied, and if God is the name for the sense of things, it is better to let the black hole where God *was* give shape to things than to admit that nothing has shape or sense. "God, however negatively conceived, explains the world." That is desperation, but understandable desperation. If God is the sense of things—a world view, if you will—to remove God is to admit utter chaos, and what is a life of utter chaos? As Kirillov said, "Man has done nothing but invent God so as to go on living, and not kill himself."

For that reason, too, people would rather attribute evil to God than deny God. Our common language experience is filled with statements about the evils God does, although it is usually not said so plainly. God takes loved ones from us in death and allows those who are able to bear it to suffer, and so on. When Kent Knutson, the President of the American Lutheran Church, died recently, a Madison, Wisconsin, pastor slammed his desk with his fist and said, "Why does God do these things to us—just when we are getting started! . . . Perhaps," he continued, "we were getting too self-confident." The religion writer who interviewed the pastor wondered whether God actively intervenes in world affairs, alternately bringing men and nations to power and toppling them again, or if, on the other hand, God just lets things go by themselves.

The first view threatens to define God as capricious and even malicious, but at least it allows one to believe that there is a divine purpose behind events, a purpose that may someday be seen as being in men's best interests. If God doesn't intervene in the world, then for all practical purposes he is dead. What good would it do to pray to a God who doesn't listen?[20]

As painful as it was to admit, the pastor and the writer both preferred to attribute evil to God rather than deny God.

The place God occupies in human life cannot simply be vacated. God-talk has not been idle talk, misguided talk, deluded talk. Talk about God, however naïve it sometimes seems to others looking in, is very near the heart of things. God has been a way to talk about the largest, most important things, about everything that is. God is a way to *see,* to know what to live for and to die for. If talk about a supernatural being cannot bear that kind of weight anymore, something else must be put in that place, something as large.

On the face of it, language about God has demonstrated bewildering variety. I would like to suggest some of the kinds of things people have meant when they said God, by no means to provide an exhaustive list but only to suggest some of the space that God-language has occupied. It is a considerable space.

"The first and most decisive presupposition of the use of the term 'God' (in the Christian sense)," Gordon Kaufman says, "is a certain metaphysical dualism or duality, an understanding of reality as distinguished into two fundamental levels or dimensions or orders: 'God' and 'the world,' the 'Creator' and 'creation.' "[21] There is no question that when most Christian people (and it is of the Western Christian tradition almost exclusively that I deal in this work) speak of God, they are at the same time affirming two kinds of things and places: this ordinary world and some other qualitatively better world. God and the company of heavenly and onetime earthly beings who accompany him are separate from this life and place. They are related levels of reality, but they are and will be finally separate. In some schemes this earth and we ourselves will be transformed into something better, but even there the two levels are distinct; before and after. Theism resides comfortably there. Theism supposes grades of being, of which we are one kind and God is another. But as Kaufman also points out, it is precisely that duality that is in question today: "The problem is whether there is *any significant reality at all* 'above' or 'beyond' or 'below' the world we know in our experience, or whether life is to be understood simply in this-worldly . . . terms."[22] If there is anything that is under fire in our historic understanding of God, it is whether something, anything, anyone, even God, exists apart from this common and mysterious place. I have already discussed theism, but it should be emphasized that while a contemporary doctrine of God must, in a sense, fill the space occupied by the older expressions of God, it is precisely the notions of some other reality alongside this one—and the idea of God as a person appropriate to that other reality—that must be rethought. If there is some other reality, we know less than nothing about it. We have imagined, as René Dubos puts it, "a Thing behind or within the thing, a Force responsible for the visible movement,"[23] and it is that Thing behind or within that is no longer believable. That is a world view within which we cannot persuade ourselves to remain or to which to return.

Sometimes when we have said God we meant to affirm a purpose or intentionality in things. "To believe in God is to believe there is a basic intentionality at work in the cosmos quite independent of man's purposive activity, and that the world and man, in the last analysis, exist for and serve these purposes of God."[24] In keeping with Christianity's pervasive theistic preferences, that purpose and intentionality has been invested in the person God. Where else, after all, except in the kind of intentionality that constitutes personhood, could purposes be invested? To speak of the intentionality or purposiveness of galaxies is simply bewildering. Belief in God the person makes it possible to affirm that galaxies do have a purpose inasmuch as God purposes, and the galaxies obey, as they must. Michael Novak says:

By belief in God, a man accepts the universe as radically personal; he believes that a Person who is the intelligent source of the world draws men, through whatever evils, to himself. By nonbelief, a man interprets the universe by an image of impersonality; of chance, of functionalism, of the laws of physics, of the absurd.[25]

Purposes are not written in the stars. Purposes are what people have. The urge to attribute purpose to a divine *person* is sound, insofar as purpose cannot be assigned to processes. But a large question arises: Is there purpose anywhere in this whole cosmic process outside of the human situation? Is there a basic intentionality at work in the cosmos independent of man, or is it man who looks at things and gives order to them? Even more, have we not, in the course of time and in the process of learning more about the universe, seen different purposes at work? Intentionality belongs to a person, quite so, but to a human person. What we accomplish by assigning cosmic intentionality to God is to affirm a particular intention for things. It is to invest ourselves completely in whatever purpose we say is God's purpose. Faced with conflicting claims for the sense of things, what outranks the assertion that *God* intends this or that? It does not matter whether I, or every Republican, or fifty million Frenchmen, or every creature that ever drew a breath thought differently; *God* intends otherwise. To invoke God always carries that kind of weight. It is to say that *nothing* matters more than whatever is being claimed. To be able to claim something *absolutely*—for that is the logical weight of God statements—is not only a denial of the uneasiness of relativity, it is security and rest. It is to *know* what, above all else, is the case. It is peace.

Sometimes talk about God functions to indicate the power, not only to give meaning but to find unity in the notorious diversity of things. "If we begin with a description of the functional significance of the encounter with the holy," Sam Keen says, "we are forced to conclude that the power to give unity and meaning to life which was once mediated by metamundane myths is today experienced as present in the principles which are the foundation of identity and community."[26] Or, similarly: "In thinking of God or the gods [men] have always meant the power in events: as when people say: *God willing.*"[27] As is the case with assertions of intention or purpose, to claim that God has the power to give unity to life is much more a comment about our own need to find wholeness and coherence than it is about life in itself or the cosmic processes.

Sometimes God has been used to affirm man's place in the universe. Roger Hazelton says that "in a real sense theology has always been anthropology, devoted to the understanding of man's place and powers in a world he never made." As a consequence, he says, it is no denial of the tradition to shift our focus "from a superbeing called God to the felt tone and texture of being human itself. . . . God," he says, "is . . . the name of the mystery of being human."[28] Or as Michael Novak puts it, "The beginning of the search for God lies in reflection upon oneself. The search for God is intimately connected with the discovery of one's own identity."[29] It is not likely that many Christians would disagree with the claim that statements about God are at the same time statements about man. The issue, though, is whether they are *only* statements about man.

Sometimes talk about God has been intended to talk about the origins of man, whether in mythological or historical ways. Sometimes God-talk defines the limits of man, sometimes man's hopes and aspirations. To speak of God as the creator probably indicates the goodness of whatever is, however infested with thorns and thistles it has become. God has been called goodness and truth and beauty. Talk about God has covered the whole arena of large human questions about who we are, and what all this means, and about the directions in which one might go.

From its beginnings and throughout its history, Christianity, in its varying traditions, has dealt with what have been usually taken to be the largest and most basic questions of human life. From it men have derived their scale of values and they have sought to fashion their way of life in the light of its teachings. It has told them of the final issues of life and death, the purpose and destiny of individuals and mankind as a whole.[30]

And God lies at the heart of that talk. Martin Buber said God was the most heavy-laden of all human words. "Generations of men have laid the burden of their anxious lives upon this word."[31]

John Smith says we can distinguish at least five different *ways* of talking about God, whatever it was we proposed to say.[32] Each way of talking is a medium through which the reality of God can be, and has been, expressed. They are the ontological, the historical, the ethical, the existential, and the linguistic. To speak of God in ontological categories is to express the true nature of being. God might, in that way, be understood theistically, as a being or, as Tillich suggests, as the power or ground of being. To speak of God in historical categories is to point to historical events and constellations of events and affirm them as God's activity in the world. Ethical categories may be used to speak of God, either as the revealer of an ethical obligation or of God as the essence of the good. God might be expressed in existential categories, by which God is the resolution of the human predicament or, to use a theology already examined, as John Robinson speaks of that utterly personal Thou that confronts us at the heart of things. Finally, God might be expressed linguistically, which would be "to find the proper structure and use of 'God-talk.' "[33]

That is to say, whatever the specific content of one's talk about God, one has at his disposal several media through which to express it. The ontological categories for describing what is meant by God are typically the media through which the early church expressed itself in its creeds: God as being, of a divine essence. The writers of the Old Testament, particularly, tended to use historical categories to make their affirmations about God: God who brought them out of Egypt, who sent Assyria to punish them, who led them to the Promised Land. Several nineteenth-century theologians spoke of God principally in ethical categories: God as the good, or Jesus as the essence of the good life, and our obligation to exemplify that goodness. Kierkegaard comes to mind as the clearest champion of existential categories for speaking of God, and I have already mentioned John Robinson's confrontation with the Thou.

The linguistic category is, I think, not parallel to the four just mentioned. It might be more apt to suggest that a linguistic search for the categories and structure of God-talk is a conscious way of looking at ontological, historical, ethical, and existential affirmations to see what is there. It is consciously to ask what is the nature and function of those, and any other, ways of talking.

The point is that Christians have made a bewildering array of statements about God—God as creator, purpose, end, hope, redeemer, truth, etc.—and that these statements have been expressed in several different categories. Talk about God as the power of history, or of God as the ground of being, are really very different ways of talking, even though *what* is being affirmed about the world or about human life may be nearly identical. The God who brought Israel out of Egypt and God as the Power of the Future are really both expressions within a historical category, past and future. Our options are open, in other words. We not only may, we probably must, sit lightly on every expression of God. But whatever the means or way or category used to speak of God, it is imperative that we ask what each assertion means in terms of the world, of society, of ourselves. If there is no otherworldly reality, then whatever the category, God-talk must be an assertion about something here, unless we are willing to charge that talk about God has been unimportant. Too many people have laid the burdens of their lives on the name to say that.

It is my intention to suggest that God-language is at least a possibility, if not even a necessity (although the name God might not be used). The problem is how to understand that universe of affirmations about God as post-Copernican people —that is, as contemporary Christians who think there is only this reality. I intend to examine a few very common but still curious statements about God to suggest ways in which talk about God can be affirmed by contemporary men in such a way that continuity with the tradition out of which we come is not severed but declared, and delighted in, and extended.

In the *Letters and Papers from Prison,* Dietrich Bonhoeffer, almost in passing, quotes a line from Euripides' play *Helen.* Helen and Menelaus have been separated for ten years, as Euripides tells the story, and really do not expect to see each other again. (The story is more complicated than that, of course, having even a spectral double for Helen, just to complicate things.) But of course they do meet, not without more complications, and when they do finally realize that a whole decade of agony and frustration is behind them, and that their most profound wishes have been realized, Helen says to Menelaus, "So then, to meet again is a god."[34]

That is a strange line, and it has been translated in a fascinating variety of ways. Without intending to suggest that a pedestrian transliteration of the original is the best translation, the original says something like "O Gods! Recognizing friends is also a god."[35] Other translations vary widely, depending on how free the translator wishes to be and how he understands the line. Richard Lattimore, for instance, translates it "O Gods!—it is divine to recognize your own."[36] Philip Vellacott has it read "O Gods! Yes, there is something godlike in recognition!"[37] There are other similar versions. I cite these, not to commend one or the other of them as the most faithful or accurate but to give some sense of the line. Since it was the Bonhoeffer version that first brought the line to my attention, I shall use it as it appears there (in what I presume is an English translation of a German version).

"So then, to meet again is a god." That is a striking sentence, mostly because we do not commonly use the word "god" that way. The issue is not monotheism versus polytheism, as if to suggest that Helen invented gods for whatever reason she needed one. Helen and Menelaus were in love in the tragic ways that Greek playwrights allowed their characters to know love. The line "to meet again is a god" is what burst out of Helen's emotions when they both realized what had happened. She might have said, "To meet again is enjoyable," but it does not take a practicing psychologist to know that that would have been not only inadequate but laughable. Or (to build a case as Ian Ramsey might have done), she might have exclaimed, "To meet again is a dream come true." That would clearly have been the case, and it would better have suited their circumstances, but she did not say that either. Helen might have said that meeting again was pure ecstasy, so wildly was her heart beating and so fast was her brain reeling, and that would have been nearer what she finally said. She said, "To meet again is a god."

While we do not usually speak that way, the logic of the line is clear. After ten years of every kind of disappointment, in which it seemed the fates themselves conspired to wear them down with disappointment, they met. And when the difficulties of recognition and the large doubts about it actually having happened were done with, Helen burst out with the largest cry people know how to make. "O Gods! Recognizing friends is also a god!" Or "To meet again is a god." It is functionally equivalent to crying out that nothing, absolutely nothing, surpasses the joy and wonder and fulfillment and ecstasy of that kind of meeting. Nothing is larger. Nothing goes deeper. Nothing matters more.

Let us use that line as a kind of paradigm—by no means an exclusive one—to inquire into the logic of talk about God.

I have a friend, Ralph, who says that Christians are idiots, that Christian morality is a mire of sentimental nonsense. Ralph says take your neighbor for all you can get. Ralph puts it somewhat more colorfully, but however earthy his language, his sentiments are clear. Ralph thinks, above all else, one should take care of oneself first, since everyone else is doing that, too, except Christians, and they are idiots. Whether Ralph actually believes that or not is not important (he doesn't act that way); Ralph says take your neighbor for all you can get.

Ralph is not unique in saying that. It is not too difficult to imagine a whole group of like-minded people who think as Ralph does (although their relationships might, if they were consistent, be pretty vicious). The whole gang might say, "Take your neighbor for all you can get." It is one thing to have just one cynical friend who says that, but it is substantially more impressive to have the whole rapacious gang say it. If all of one's regular comrades advocated a philosophy like that, it is likely that we should give more attention to the creed they profess than if only Ralph advocated it.

Let us imagine that fifty million Frenchmen advocate taking one's neighbor for all one can get. Fifty million Frenchmen is a lot of people, and if fifty million Frenchmen agree that the neighbor is there to be *had,* something substantial and respectable might be at stake.

And, for the sake of argument at least, one could imagine that absolutely everybody else agrees and advocates plundering your neighbor. It would be very hard to withstand that kind of unanimity.

However, even if I were all alone, and I believed that God wanted me to love my neighbor, the claim of God on my life would be larger than a conflicting claim from Ralph, the whole gang, fifty million Frenchmen, or absolutely everybody else. If God says, Love your neighbor, and if I believe that, then insofar as my conviction can find strength, I will reject every other conflicting demand and try to love my neighbor. "God" carries that kind of weight. Christians have always believed that.

In the logic of a pre-Copernican world view or, more precisely, in the logic of a Judeo-Christian pre-Copernican world view, to believe that "God says love your neighbor" is to think that God, the divine person of every kind of power and wisdom and magnificence, to whom we owe our whole being, wants us to love our neighbor. No one else, not even everyone else, can make that kind of claim on us. Nothing matters more than God. The logic of God-language and God-claims upon us is clear. The problem is that fewer and fewer people can seriously reinvest themselves in that world view, a world view with this reality and another reality alongside this one where God is, where we shall someday be.

I suggested earlier that I did not care to describe the difference in world views as a religious versus a secular world view. One is put into the position of denying the wrong things by accepting the terms that way. It is, to use Kee's term, a little like being an a-unicornist. But the issue here, to use "secular" language for a moment, is the one Dietrich Bonhoeffer raised during World War II: "How do we speak in a secular way about 'God'?" How can we affirm what our fathers affirmed without having to live in their world view, too? Living there is simply impossible for anyone who does not see that way any longer.

Most Westerners spend most of their time in a post-Copernican world, at least for most things. We don't act as if this were a three-storied universe, with the earth in the middle. We have let hell as a place go, and perhaps heaven too, although very commonly religious people want to affirm both, if not as places then as states of present or future being or some such thing (whatever that could mean). But not many of us believe in devils and imps as the causes of illnesses or mischief. Not many of us believe that Satan is a being, although we might want to assert something about radical evil. Commonly, we have pared that older world view down until practically only God remains: a supernatural person, absolute, holy, eternal, righteous, gracious, and so on. And insofar as one believes God like that is there, he still lives in an older world view. God is the essence of that world view.

Bonhoeffer asked whether we could speak of God without that world view. Bonhoeffer tried, but he did not accomplish it. For the most part, he resorted to paradox, and paradoxes are more a statement of dilemma than of resolution. Is it possible to affirm what our fathers affirmed without having to move into their universe? To do that, one thing must be kept clearly in mind: "God" cannot mean a supernatural being in a supernatural world somehow alongside or above or within our world. And if God-talk is not about a superperson, it must be about this world, about our lives together, about me.

Recall again the line from Euripedes' *Helen:* "To meet again is a god." I suggested that Helen was talking not about an incidental member of a divine family of beings but about her meeting with Menelaus. It was the largest kind of statement she could make about their meeting. It wasn't just pleasant or even astonishing: it was a god! All the possible comparisons drop away. It was like saying that even though Ralph and fifty million Frenchmen and everybody says otherwise, God says love your neighbor. Nothing supersedes the magnitude of that statement. Let me state it this way: the statement "God says love one another" is functionally equivalent to saying "to love one another is a god." In both cases, a claim has been made about loving one another. In both cases one has said the equivalent of this: that *nothing* matters more than that we love one another. In both cases the person who speaks the line, who affirms that faith, will commit himself to loving his neighbor in ways that, for all practical purposes, will look pretty much like that of the other person. Both persons will organize their lives in order to care for the neighbor. Both will lament their inability to live out their beliefs completely (for both of them share human weaknesses and perversity, too). People committed to the same ends, holding the same philosophy, or sharing a common faith, almost always show diversity of means toward the end they share, but other than that, nothing in the behavior of the two people we have been imagining will distinguish them.

There is one great difference between them. The person who says "God says love one another" sees reality differently than the person who says "To love one another is a god." Their world views are different. For the former, God is a personal being to whom all of creation owes its being and its destiny, and whose command therefore is without parallel. For the latter, there is no person "out there," no supernatural reality at all, but by commitment the neighbor is to be loved above all else.

I said earlier that both statements are functionally equivalent to saying that nothing matters more than that we love one another. We could say then that we have three ways of saying the same thing:

1. The theist might say, "God says love one another."
2. Another, still using the term "god" but not intending to imagine any reality apart from this one, might say, "To love one another is a god."
3. A third, wishing to avoid even the term "god" but intending to affirm the same understanding of life, might say, "Nothing matters more than that we love one another."

Let us use another example. Christians have traditionally said something like "God is just," or "God wills justice." Within the framework of a pre-Copernican world view in which God was conceived of as a person, those statements entailed a logic something like this: It is of the very essence of God's being that he is just. To know justice is to know God. We are his creation, made in his image, intended to be finite embodiments of his virtues. We therefore should be just, holding justice alongside love (of which similar things are said) as our highest commitment. Presumably, insofar as we are able, we will attempt to incarnate justice.

The nontheist cannot conceive of reality that way, although he may indeed believe that justice is of the very essence of things, or better, that justice is his highest commitment (perhaps also alongside love). If he wishes to avoid God-talk altogether, he might say that nothing matters more than doing justice. Or, if he uses God-language nontheistically, he might say that to do justice is a god. Again, in all three cases, the lives that eventuate from that commitment, however one says it, however one sees "reality" (that is, whether one- or three-storied), will be the same. All three will live and die for the realization of justice in their own lives and in the world. Justice will be the commitment beyond which they have no

other, although there may be commitments *alongside* justice:
love or peace, for instance. We have traditionally said that
God is love, or that God is just, or that God wills peace. In
other words, we do not say love is God, or justice is God, or
that peace is God. We have said God is many things. We have
not elevated one virtue, but we proclaim a whole vision of life.

One might object that the kinds of God-talk I have proposed so far are inadequate to carry the full weight of what
God has meant. Most strikingly, the idea of God as a personal being is entirely missing, just as the reality or existence
of anything beyond this ordinary reality is gone. But that is
precisely what we have proposed to try to do. To borrow
Bonhoeffer's question again: Is it possible to speak in a secular way about "God"? I have proposed to try that because,
for increasing numbers of people, resort to some other reality
to explain this one is simply unbelievable. I am arguing that,
with that deliberate and necessary exception, one can speak
of the things Christians have always committed themselves to
with the same breadth and depth our fathers claimed. Just as
it is clearly the case that great numbers of contemporary
people—post-Copernican people—cannot think of the natural
world and themselves in terms of a supernatural realm, so are
there many Christians who cannot think of the natural world
without resort to another realm to explain this one. So it will
be the case, then, that for many, many people Bonhoeffer's
question is answered almost before it is asked. They simply
deny the attempt to speak of God only in terms of this world
precisely because they are committed to belief in a world
view in which God as a person is the essence of their way of
seeing things. They can *say* Bonhoeffer's question, but they
cannot *conceive* it. It is as impossible for them to imagine
things without God as a person as it is for others to conceive
of a supernatural reality alongside the natural world.

What is at stake, then, is a conflict of world views. That is
why, if we are going to speak of God in a "secular" way, God
cannot be spoken of as a personal being. God as a personal
being is of the very essence of an earlier, although severely
amputated, world view. The question is how to speak of God
without seeing that way. But precisely because world views
are a way of "seeing" everything, it will be the case, and

clearly *is* the case, that many people will not be able to see any way other than the way they do. Only for those who simply do not see as they earlier did (or their fathers earlier did), or for those who find their "reality" coming apart, will it be possible openly to consider whether the kinds of things I am proposing here are adequate. Anyone who suggests that God must be a personal being is simply affirming that he holds an older world view, one which I, for instance, can no longer live in.

For the same reasons, the charge that what I propose here is simply a reduction to ethics is a misunderstanding of what is being said. Our fathers in the faith, I am suggesting, affirmed precisely what we can affirm about the things we can do as human beings (ethics). In addition, they grounded those ethics in a world view in which they posited God and Satan and a host of other beings and places. Just so do we ground our ethics in a world view, although it is quite another view. In that sense, this is no reduction, just an alternative way of seeing.

Nor is this a reduction to Jesus. I do not propose to eliminate talk about God but to understand and affirm it in the ways it can be affirmed within a subsequent world view. To reduce religion to Jesus would be to suggest that God-talk was simply nonsense, and that is not so. Whether in terms of an ancient world view or a more recent one, Jesus *is* terribly important. In both cases Jesus is usually affirmed as the incarnation, the embodiment, of those things one is committed to. And Jesus *is* definitive for the Christian community in the sense that, without him, there would be no church and that to this day the church is the community that defines itself as the people in whom Jesus "lives."

A thank-you note appeared in a semipublic newsletter some time ago that demonstrates, in a different way, the possibilities of understanding talk about God within the contexts of separate world views. The family concerned had undergone more difficulty than any family could bear, were tragedies known beforehand. But they were, and are, magnificently strong people, and they sent a note of appreciation to the whole community in which the husband works. "The moral and spiritual support demonstrated by all of you," he wrote, "has been a gift of God to us during this time."

Within the context of a world view that understands God to be a supernatural person who, directly or indirectly, affects the course of events within this natural world, that note of appreciation is consistently meaningful. God, directly or through the working of his Spirit, or through his Son who lives in Christian people, in ways that are almost entirely mysterious to limited natural experience, causes people to do good and kind and helpful things; Christians usually say God "inspires" them to commendable behavior. In this case, the moral and spiritual support demonstrated by those people seemed to the injured family to be such a gift of God.

Those kinds of human activities happen, whatever the manner in which people put reality together; people do usually care, and often show their concern. The question is how that demonstration of concern shall be interpreted. What is the nature of reality? Without changing a word, the same note might be understood with quite a different logic. Even if one has concluded that there is no supernatural sphere, and no person anywhere who corresponds to the name God, still one might say, somewhat in the manner of Helen's statement to Menelaus, "Your moral and spiritual support has been a gift of God to us." In effect, the question was: How much has your demonstrated concern mattered to us? Not just a little. Not even quite a lot. It has been "a gift of God to us." It mattered beyond telling. There is no larger way to say how much it mattered.

Had the letter writer wanted to, had it been his intention to speak without God-language, he might have said, "Nothing could have mattered more to us than your demonstrated concern," or some such thing. In every instance, the empirical facts remain the same: accident, concern shown, expression of profound gratitude. The variable factor is the world view that lies behind the alternative ways of speaking. The kindness and the gratitude are not changed by a shift in world views, only the way one "sees" and talks about it.

It often happens that Christians interpret events in their lives as actions of God, who may or may not act directly, but who seems often to work through human and nonhuman activities. One of my friends, named Joe, described the time in his life when, more certainly than any other time, God seemed to act through him.

It was August. We were on vacation with my parents at our family cabin on a remote lake in northern Minnesota. The morning was glorious. The lake was calm. The sky was a pale blue with enormous billowy clouds: an idyllic day.

In the cabin, however, a storm was gathering. My sister had just returned from a visit to my older brother, a parish pastor in a small town in Montana. As she related details of her visit, my father began to think about a college loan my brother had never repaid him.

Largely out of a sense of annoyance at having a vacation morning disturbed, I sat down and wrote a long letter to my brother. I described a beautiful day ruined. I spoke of our father; offended because his son refused to pay anything on the loan or even to respond when Father had mentioned the matter in several letters. I spoke of our mother's hope that they could visit them in the fall, and of my father's angry response: "Not until he does something about that loan."

I never did receive a response to that letter. But my father received a five-page letter in which my older brother shared all of the details of his financial situation: his salary, his family costs, his debts, and a pointed statement indicating why on his salary he could not pay off the loan at the present time.

That was all my father needed. In the fall my parents spent a full week of vacation with my older brother and his family. I have been told that before the week was over, my father cancelled the loan. My parents returned full of praise for the "Big Sky Country."

In early March the following spring, I had an early morning telephone call from my father telling of a bad traffic accident. My mother was hospitalized with severe internal injuries. She died a day later, and I made a telephone call to my brother in Montana. He and his family left immediately and were with us a day later to comfort my father.

It was when I saw my father and my brother comforting each other that I thought again about my letter. And the thought went through my head: if God has ever acted in my life, it was then.

I am not sure how Joe intended his statement that God acted through him when he wrote an angry letter. It does not matter. Either way the meaning is clear. If he were thinking that God even uses family quarrels and angry letters to cause fathers and sons to learn to care for each other, then God acted in that sad and summer time.

I pressed Joe about his story. What do you mean, "If God ever acted, it was then"? Joe replied that if there ever were a time when he felt most satisfyingly *human,* most as he believed human beings ought to be with each other, it was then. Joe is committed to a vision of life as he finds it in the Judeo-Christian tradition. Once, at least once, Joe realized beyond all other times what it meant to realize that vision. It was not just a satisfying act, it was an act of God. It was not just a *good* time, it was a time from God.

Reconciling friends is also a god.

I have been arguing that talk about God is intimately bound up with our most deep-seated convictions about life. God is the largest way we can say those things. In a chapel talk he called "Beth's Prayer," Paul Hjelle, who is a campus pastor at Luther College, described how his three-year-old daughter found the logic of "God."

She had been put to bed (several times) and the ritual of several drinks of water had been carried out. After she was tucked into bed supposedly for the last time, she called out once more. I went to her room again, with discipline in mind. She said, "I want to say my prayers." She had already said her prayers, but I thought perhaps she had forgotten someone.

She began: "God, I know you love all little children, *so,* can I play with Ronnie tomorrow?" Then she replied, *"Yes."* "God, I know you love little animals, *so,* can I sleep with my bear?" *"Yes."*[38]

To whom should a three-year-old theologian appeal who wants to play with Ronnie tomorrow? Where do Christians of all ages in every age find their strongest affirmations of the rightness of things, even of the goodness of sleeping with bears? Beth *knew* how God-language worked. With a faith adequate to move mountains and melt the firmest father's